D0521973

THE COMMONSENSE
INDIAN
COOKERY BOOK

THE COMMONSENSE INDIAN COOKERY BOOK

SARA MATHEWS

ANGUS & ROBERTSON PUBLISHERS

All measurements conform to the metric cup and spoon measurements of the Standards Association of Australia. British and American readers please note that:

1 metric cup 250 ml.
1 tablespoon 20 ml.
1 teaspoon 5 ml.

Spoon measures are *level* spoonfuls.

Angus & Robertson Publishers
London • Sydney • Melbourne • Singapore
Manila

First published by Angus & Robertson Publishers, Australia, 1977
Reprinted 1983 by The Thetford Press Ltd., Thetford, Norfolk

© Sara Mathews 1977

National Library of Australia
card number and ISBN 0 207 13450 2

PREFACE

Cooking can be great fun. With a little practice anyone can cook a meal to be proud of, and, as soon as a few basic methods have been learnt, and the use of some spices mastered, can also create his or her own exciting recipes.

I hope that this book will be an inspiring and practical introduction to Indian-style cooking for beginner and experienced cook alike. **Please read the section 'How to Use This Book' (p. 2) and chapter The Art of Indian Cookery (p. 3), before you try any of the recipes.**

The most important thing in good cooking—especially Indian cooking where there are no hard and fast rules—is imagination. So relax and enjoy yourself in the kitchen—I have found that this is the best way to ensure interesting and delicious results!

May I take this opportunity to thank Dr Vimala, my husband Mathews, son Mohan and daughter-in-law Linda for their constant help and encouragement while I was preparing this book.

Sara Mathews

FOREWORD

Sara Mathews was born of Yemani parents in Singapore, and hence has spent many years in a place where people of different races and different countries intermingle; where one can find restaurants and eating houses that serve both superb Indian, Chinese, South-east Asian and European food. It is no wonder that she can turn her hand to any sort of cooking!

I have long been waiting to lay my hands on some of Sara Mathews' recipes. The first time we ever had the good fortune to taste some of her cooking, all of us including the children were immediately captivated. The subtle aroma of spices used in the right quantities, and the variety of dishes that were prepared—one complementing the other—showed a talent that not many possess. But she assures us and shows us in the pages that follow, that it is not too difficult for even the least gifted amongst us to acquire similar skills. She has shown that all those exotic eastern dishes can be easily prepared by any one of us—a beginner—by following a few basic directions. Also, one is not intimidated by a long list of foreign-sounding spices and herbs that have never been seen or heard of in this country. All the spices and herbs listed are available in supermarkets, delicatessens, health food stores and shops specialising in Indian foodstuffs. A visit to one of these stores—a little planning and imagination and *voila*! Mrs Mathews shows you how to turn your kitchen into the centre of Eastern cuisine!

Dr Vimala Nayanar

DEDICATION

In memory of my mother, Rachel S. Syed,
who taught me to cook and to love cooking.

CONTENTS

Note: Before trying the recipes please read the section, How to Use This Book [p. 2].

ILLUSTRATIONS

INTRODUCTION

This book is intended for those who enjoy Indian-style food and wish to cook it for themselves, their family and friends. All the ingredients used are readily available in supermarkets, grocery stores and shops specialising in spices or Eastern foods, and the instructions are given in simple, step-by-step form so that beginner and experienced cook alike can achieve delicious results.

As I lived for many years in Singapore, where one can experience every type of Asian cookery, some of my favourite recipes are inspired by Chinese, Malay, Persian, and Arabian cookery. I have included these recipes here, as not only are they delicious and colourful, but they combine beautifully with pure Indian food, and will add variety of flavour, appearance and texture to your dinner parties.

It is not necessary to buy a wide range of exotic ingredients, perhaps used only occasionally, in order to use the recipes in this book. I have given a basic list of spices and foods commonly used in Indian cookery on p. 6. Those marked with an asterisk (*) are those used most often. If you have these on hand, you will be able to make up most of these recipes. Later, you may wish to expand your store.

Where possible, I have suggested alternatives to spices and foods which you may not have in your store cupboard. If no alternative is mentioned in the recipe itself, check the basic ingredients list (p. 6) where possible substitutions are listed after the description of each foodstuff. Substitutions will not always give the same flavour to a dish as the original ingredients, but they will go part of the way towards it. The exception to this is the substitution of evaporated milk for cream of coconut. Obviously these flavours are not similar. The alternative is intended for people who do not like the taste of coconut—the evaporated milk balances the recipe and gives a creamy effect without a strong coconut flavour.

HOW TO USE THIS BOOK

These recipes are attractive and delicious in themselves, but also are simple introductions to Indian-style cookery. They introduce basic spice combinations and cooking techniques, and the interested cook can go on to experiment with different combinations of spices in different ratios—not necessarily to cook an Indian curry, but perhaps to give lamb chops, steak, a roast, minced steak or even sausages a different, special flavour.

I must stress that these are recipes in their *basic* form. The quantities of spices given are small, so that people who are familiar with, and enjoy, highly-spiced food will almost certainly wish to increase the amounts by half, one or even two or three times. On the other hand, people who like the flavour and aroma of spices, but either do not like or cannot tolerate very highly-spiced dishes, may use the quantities as given, or reduce them, and omit the chilli.

Please note that the amounts of cooking oil and water, and any cooking times given in the recipes are approximate only. Don't be afraid to add more oil or fluid or to vary cooking time. Different cuts of meat, different cooking pots, different stoves, the juiciness of any vegetables used, and many other factors affect cooking times and the amounts of cooking medium needed.

I have suggested the number of serves each recipe produces, but please regard these suggestions *as* suggestions, not hard and fast rules. Appetites vary. Also, if several curries are served at one time, serves of each individual curry are smaller than if that curry is the only dish on the table. You should use your judgment on this matter, using my suggested number of serves as a guide.

I have given quantities in metric and imperial measure. The metric and imperial measures are not exact equivalents—I have rounded numbers, making 1 lb the alternative to 500 g when in fact it is slightly less, for example. But none of the recipes will be affected by this small variation.

THE ART OF INDIAN COOKING

The secret of fine Indian cooking is the subtle blending of meats, vegetables and spices to create dishes of many different types and flavours, from fiery hot curries to tangy, spiced dishes and mild curries and grills in which just a suggestion of spices bring out the flavour of the meat.

A simple Indian meal may consist of a meat, a fish and a chicken dish with rice or bread, a salad and a vegetable dish, and chutney. A more elaborate menu may contain extra meat dishes, more salads, and extra chutneys, and a pudding or sweet may be served at the end of the meal. In this book you will find recipes for savoury dishes, to serve before the main meal or with drinks or afternoon tea, Indian breads, fish and prawn dishes, chicken and duck dishes, lamb, beef and pork dishes, vegetables, salads, rice dishes, chutneys, pickles and sauces, and Indian desserts.

COOKING METHODS

A large number of Indian dishes begin with the frying of onion and spices. The main ingredient (meat, fish, chicken, vegetables) is then added, perhaps with a little liquid, and boiled or simmered until cooked. Long, slow cooking, and the addition of the smallest possible amount of liquid enables the spices to mix and release their full flavour, to penetrate the other ingredients thoroughly, and, if the curry is a 'wet' one, create a delicious gravy. Do not be tempted to add extra spices to the dish at the end of the cooking, to adjust the flavour. They will taste 'raw', and spoil the curry.

I have not given definite cooking times here as these can vary so much depending on ingredients, type of stove and pan and many other conditions, but often you will note the instruction, 'cook until oil rises'—here you should look for spots of oil on the surface of the curry, indicating that the dish or stage is nearing completion.

EQUIPMENT

In India, some people use only earthenware pots for cooking. Each pot is used for only one type of curry—meat, fish, chicken and so on. The flavours gradually permeate the pot and improve the taste of following curries. Other people use only metal cooking pots and utensils—at one time brass was used, but now stainless steel is very popular. Indian food has been cooked with very simple utensils for thousands of years, and you do not need any special or elaborate equipment to prepare it in your own kitchen, but the following items are useful:

A kwali or wok (Chinese cooking pan), and/or an electric frypan or large, heavy frying pan.

A small frying pan, for the quick cooking of garnishes, extra onion, and so on.

One or more large, heavy-bottomed cooking pots with tight-fitting lids—ideally these should be able to be put in the oven, and into the refrigerator, when necessary. Many types of casserole dishes can be used in this way, and used for serving too!

Wooden spoons of various sizes.

Mortar and pestle, for grinding spices.

Electric blender, for blending chutneys, making spice pastes and sauces.

A set of good knives, for chopping meat and vegetables.

One or more wooden chopping boards.

Mixing bowls of various sizes.

A marble slab and rolling pin, for bread making.

COOKING MEDIUMS

Traditionally, ghee, or clarified butter, has been used in Indian cookery, giving a delicious, rich taste to the food. Today, however, more people, especially in Western countries, are using vegetable oils, particularly the polyunsaturated varieties, in cooking. These oils are lighter and thought to be better for the health than cooking mediums which are high in saturated fats.

For this reason, I have specified cooking oil throughout this book, unless the use of ghee or butter is necessary or desirable to achieve good results. This is a matter of choice and taste, however, and ghee, butter, margarine or oils such as peanut, sunflower and safflower may all be used as desired. Olive oil is not used in Indian cookery, nor is lard.

In the following recipes I have specified the minimum quantities of cooking oil and water. Do not hesitate to add extra if you feel it is necessary, or if you wish to make a 'dry' curry into a 'wet' one by creating a gravy. Remember, however, that too much water will make a watery gravy, and add extra little by little, and with care.

SPICES

Many people just beginning to cook Asian food find the idea of working with many strange spices rather daunting. But in fact a few of the spices will be quite familiar—cloves and cinnamon, for example, and perhaps chilli, paprika and ginger—and the interested cook will soon learn to recognise and work confidently with cummin, coriander, turmeric, cardamom and the rest.

Spices should be as fresh as possible. It has been assumed in the recipes that most spices are to be used in powder form. They can be bought by weight at health food stores and shops which specialise in Indian foods, or, more expensively, in jars and packets in supermarkets and grocery stores. If you intend to use the spices infrequently, buy only a small quantity at a time. Keep spices in tightly capped jars, to keep them fresh.

When using spices remember that they need to be cooked to produce their rich, distinctive flavours. As noted above, it is unwise to add extra spices at the end of the cooking, in order to change or correct the taste of the dish—the spices will taste 'raw' and will conflict with the tastes of the cooked spices in the curry.

BASIC INGREDIENTS

Those ingredients marked with an asterisk (*) are used very commonly, and should be used as the basis of a store of Indian spices and foods.

Almonds: nuts which are ground and used in several Indian dishes, and also used whole, chopped and slivered as a garnish. May be bought with or without skins, whole, halved, chopped or slivered.

*Black pepper: may be bought as small, black peppercorns and used whole or freshly ground, or as powder.

Bay leaves: dried leaves of the bay laurel tree, used in flavouring many foods. Substitute: small sprig coriander leaves for 1 bay leaf. Note: substitution will alter flavour.

Besan flour: lentil flour available in some health food shops and shops specialising in Indian foods.

Blackgram flour: another type of lentil flour.

*Cardamom: an important curry spice, strong and aromatic, available as pods and powder. Substitute: 2 cardamom pods, crushed, for $\frac{1}{4}$ teaspoon powder, and vice versa.

Capsicum: or green pepper. Related to chillies, but lacking most of their hotness. May be used as a substitute for fresh green chillies in many dishes. Substitute: 2 green chillies for 1 small capsicum, although these will give a hotter result.

*Chilli: available as fresh, green chillies, dried red chillies, chilli powder, and chilli paste. Chilli gives colour, flavour and heat to most Indian-style dishes. Those who are not used to hot foods should use only a little chilli at first, and gradually increase the quantity used, if desired. Chilli can be omitted entirely, if desired —the recipes will work quite well without it, though will not be quite so tasty. Substitute: 1 small capsicum for 2 green chillies, 2 tablespoons chilli paste for 2 tablespoons chilli powder, and vice versa.

Chilli sauce: a hot sauce useful as a dip for meat balls and so on. May be used in place of chilli paste in an emergency. Substitute: as a dip, tabasco sauce or tomato sauce. Note: flavours are different.

Cinnamon: available as bark (cinnamon stick) or powder. An important curry spice, aromatic warm and sweet in taste. Substitute: 15 mm ($\frac{1}{2}$ in) cinnamon stick, crushed, for $\frac{1}{4}$ teaspoon cinnamon powder and vice versa.

Cloves: available whole or powdered. An important curry spice, strongly aromatic and pungent.

Coconut cream: concentrated coconut, also called creamed coconut, and cream of coconut, available in many supermarkets and shops specialising in Indian foodstuffs, often in the refrigerated section. Used as is or dissolved in water. Store in refrigerator. Substitute: for liquid coconut cream, equal quantity canned coconut milk *or* evaporated milk. Note: evaporated milk substitution will change flavour of dish.

Coconut milk: available in cans or may be made by dissolving coconut cream in water 30 g–60 g (1 oz–2 oz) coconut cream to every $\frac{1}{2}$ cup water, depending on thickness required. Substitute: for every $\frac{1}{2}$ cup coconut milk, $\frac{1}{2}$ cup evaporated milk in which 30 g–60 g (1 oz–2 oz) desiccated coconut has been soaked and strained out *or* plain evaporated milk. Note: substitutions will change flavour of dish.

Coconut, desiccated: dried grated coconut, used in some curries and Indian desserts, for making coconut milk, some chutneys, and salads.

Coriander: used extensively in seed and powder form—a gentle, fragrant spice, an important curry ingredient which rounds and balances the hotter spices. Coriander leaves are often used as a garnish in Indian cooking, and as an ingredient in salads, chutneys and some curries. Coriander is easily grown in a pot. It is also known as Chinese parsley. Substitution: for powder: equal quantity curry powder; for fresh leaves: celery leaves.

Cummin: an important curry ingredient with a warm, aromatic taste. Available in powder form.

Curry powder: blended curry spices. Mixture may be mild or hot according to recipe. Commercial curry powders are available, but these do not give the fine flavour of a home-made curry mixture. A commercial preparation, however, may be used as a substitute for coriander powder, if necessary.

Curry paste: a paste made of blended curry spices, generally giving superior results to the commercial curry powders.

Curry leaves: small leaves, available dried for addition to curries.

Evaporated milk: I use this as a substitute for coconut milk when I am cooking for someone who does not like coconut. Also gives creamy taste to desserts. Substitute: fresh milk, especially creamy milk.

Fenugreek: seeds used whole or ground in curries. Powder also available. Strong aroma and slightly bitter taste. Use in small quantities.

*Garam Masala: a mixture of several spices, often used at the end of cooking. Strong perfume. May be bought already mixed where spices are sold, or made at home by following this recipe:

> 20 g ($\frac{3}{4}$ oz) cardamom seeds
> 20 g ($\frac{3}{4}$ oz) cinnamon stick
> 7 g ($\frac{1}{4}$ oz) black cummin seed
> 3 pinches mace
> 3 pinches nutmeg powder
> Grind first 4 ingredients together to make a smooth powder. Add nutmeg, mix, and store in air-tight jar.

*Garlic: a pungent bulb which will separate into several cloves, peeled, and crushed, pounded or chopped to add flavour to all types of food. Substitute: $\frac{1}{4}$ teaspoon garlic powder for 1 clove fresh garlic.

*Ginger: the root of a tropical plant, available fresh, powdered and canned. Preserved, sugared ginger is used as a sweetmeat. My recipes specify fresh ginger, which should be scraped before being pounded or shredded. Vary the amount of ginger used to suit your taste. It has a strong, distinctive flavour, so should be used with care at first. Substitute: $\frac{1}{4}$ teaspoon ginger powder for 1 thin slice fresh ginger.

Ghee: the clarified butter in which Indian food has been traditionally cooked. Substitute: as cooking medium, cooking oil, butter, margarine; in bread and dessert making: butter or margarine.

Lemon grass: a fragrant herb which may be bought in dried form or grown in the garden.

Lime juice: fresh juice of the lime, a member of the citrus family. Substitute: for 1 tablespoon lime juice, 1 tablespoon vinegar mixed with one teaspoon sugar *or* equal quantity fresh lemon juice.

Mint: a refreshing, tangy herb used in salads and chutneys, as a curry ingredient, and as a garnish. Easy to grow in pot or garden, also available in dried form, chopped.

Monosodium glutamate: a food additive of vegetable origin, used extensively in Chinese cooking to bring out the flavour of food. It is sold under various brand names. Use in very small amounts.

Mustard seed: used whole or crushed in curries; has a strong, hot flavour and is usually used in small quantities.

Nutmeg: a pungent spice, available whole or in powder form.

*Onion: sliced or chopped onion, fried golden brown, is used as the base for most curries. The frying caramelises the sugar in the onion, to release the delicious flavour and aroma. Onion rings, fried or raw, are commonly used as garnish, and onion is also used extensively in salads. Substitute: as curry ingredient, dried onion flakes are available, but do not give as good a result as fresh onion; as garnish, spring onions and shallots.

Pappadums: paper-thin lentil cakes which may be bought in packets at supermarkets and specialty stores. When fried in hot oil they swell, curl and double their size. Used as curry accompaniment or savoury.

Paprika: a member of the chilli family, red spice with full, hot flavour, but lacking heat of chilli powder.

* *Rice*: brown and white, served with curry or as base for dishes such as pilaus and biryanis. See Rice chapter for further information. Rice flour is used in the making of pancakes, fritters and other starchy foods.

Raisins: dried fruit commonly used in chutneys and in curries, particularly as a garnish, usually fried until swollen. Substitute: as garnish, in some dishes, sultanas.

Sago: grain commonly used to make puddings and sweets.

Semolina: grain commonly used to make puddings and sweets.

Sesame oil: a fragrant oil obtained from the sesame seed, used extensively in Chinese cooking. Use in very small quantities.

Shallots: a member of the onion family, leaves and stalk used extensively as garnish and in salads in Indian cooking, and common ingredients in Chinese. Substitute: spring onions.

Soy sauce: made from soy beans, very extensively used in Chinese cooking as ingredient and condiment.

Stock cubes: concentrated beef, chicken, onion or fish flavouring, mixed with water or added crumbled to many dishes to create richer flavour.

Tamarind: pulp from the pod of the tamarind tree, used in making tamarind water, a common curry ingredient. To make tamarind water, soak a piece of tamarind (about a tablespoon) in $\frac{1}{2}$ cup hot water and allow to stand for 15 minutes. Strain water into another container, squeezing tamarind pulp as dry as possible. Discard pulp. Use more tamarind pulp if a stronger, more sour taste is required. Substitute: for $\frac{1}{2}$ cup tamarind water, $1\frac{1}{2}$ tablespoons tamarind paste or 2 tablespoons lime or lemon juice *or* $\frac{1}{2}$ cup vinegar.

* *Tamarind paste*: a convenient method of adding tamarind to curry, used alone or mixed with water to make tamarind water. Substitute: for 1 tablespoon tamarind paste 6 tablespoons tamarind water *or* $1\frac{1}{2}$ tablespoons lime or lemon juice *or* 3 tablespoons vinegar.

* *Turmeric*: a golden-yellow fragrant spice extensively used to colour and flavour curries, vegetables, rice and savouries. Substitute: saffron.

* *Yoghurt*: milk curd, used in its natural form both as a curry ingredient and a curry accompaniment, plain, spiced or with cucumber. Yoghurt may be purchased or made at home. It must be kept in the refrigerator.

ENTERTAINING

An Indian dinner party usually consists of several main dishes—meat, fish and chicken—a vegetable or two, salads, bread or rice, yoghurt, pappadums and several chutneys and pickles. The dishes are placed in the centre of the table, and the guests help themselves. This, and the fact that most of the dishes can be eaten with a fork, make Indian food very suitable for a buffet meal or a large party.

Here are a few points to remember when choosing dishes to serve:

Serve dishes and chutneys and pickles of varying hotness. Not everyone likes or can eat very hot, spicy food.

Serve some 'dry' and some 'wet' dishes, so there will not be too much or too little gravy.

Serve plain rice with rich dishes like Pork Balls in Yoghurt Sauce, leaving the more elaborate rice dishes for plainer food, like Kababs.

Pappadums and yoghurt may be served with any combination of dishes.

If you wish to serve bread, but do not wish to make your own, any crusty, uncut loaf will substitute. Serve warm.

There should be plenty to drink with the meal—cold water, fruit juices, soft drinks, wine or cold beer.

The menus set out below vary from the simple, suitable for a light lunch, to the more elaborate, for a dinner party. Recipes for all the dishes are in this book, and the number of dishes may be increased or reduced, as desired. These menus are, of course, only a few of the hundreds of possibilities, but I hope they will give you some ideas.

SUGGESTED MENUS

MENU 1
Chapati *or* Puris *or* Bread
Pork in Tomato
Spiced Cauliflower
Green Apple Chutney
Lychees with Mixed Fruits

MENU 2
Brown or White Rice
Pork Curry
Spiced Mixed Vegetables
Tomato Salad
Apple and Pineapple Chutney
Melon Dessert

MENU 3
White Rice
Minced Meat Curry
Red Lentils
Cabbage in Coconut
Cucumber and Pineapple Salad
Lemon and Date Pickle
Banana Coconut Pudding

MENU 4
Rice with Red Lentils
Mild Chicken Curry
Spiced Aubergine
Cucumber and Tomato Salad
Lemon Pickle
Fruit Salad with Almond Jelly

MENU 5
Chapati *or* Puris *or* Bread
Lamb Sambal
Zucchini and Potatoes
Cucumber, Onion and Celery Salad
Spiced Yoghurt
Pappadums
Mint Chutney
Sweet Potato Pudding

MENU 6
Yellow Rice
Beef or Lamb with Coconut
Fried Chicken Wings
Mixed Vegetable Curry
Cucumber and Tomato Salad
Lychees with Honeydew Melon

MENU 7
Persian Rice
Beef Ball Curry
Chicken in Spicy Sauce
Spiced Aubergine
Lemon and Date Pickle
Spiced Mixed Vegetables
Yoghurt with Cucumber
Mixed Fruit Salad

MENU 8
Tomato Rice
Kurmah
Savoury Prawns
Kashmir Chilli Chicken
Egg Curry with Potatoes
Cucumber and Pineapple Salad
Vermicelli Pudding

MENU 9
Coconut Rice
Beef Malaysian Style
Minced Meat Cake
Chicken Baked in Curry Sauce
Fish with Fresh Chillies and Tamarind
Vegetable Salad
Lychees with Mixed Fruit

MENU 10
Egg Pilau
Minced Meat Curry
Chicken in Tomato
Prawns in Coconut
Fish Cakes
Zucchini and Potatoes
Cucumber, Onion and Celery Salad
Green Apple Chutney
Sago and Sweet Potato Pudding

SAVOURIES

This chapter contains recipes for savoury foods to serve with drinks, before dinner, as snacks or suppers, or with afternoon tea, as they are in India. The fritters and meat and fish balls may be prepared ahead of time, left uncooked and fried at the last minute, or cooked and warmed on a baking tray in a medium oven (uncovered) when required, if desired.

Many other recipes in following chapters are also, of course, very suitable for use as a first course or savoury, so experiment with these also. And some of the savoury dishes may be used as main course dishes, also, especially when several dishes are being served.

If you have no time to prepare foods to serve before your Indian meal, offer your guests a selection of raw vegetables, such as carrot sticks, celery curls, spring onions and tiny radishes, or simply make big bowls of pappadums (p. 23), which are delicious to nibble with drinks as well as accompanying curries.

PRAWN FRITTERS

500 g (1 lb) small cooked prawns, shelled
$\frac{1}{2}$ cup rice flour
$\frac{1}{2}$ cup self-raising flour
1 tablespoon cornflour
1 teaspoon baking powder
$\frac{1}{2}$ cup semolina flour
$\frac{1}{2}$ cup besan flour
1 large onion, chopped finely
Thin slice ginger, chopped finely
$\frac{1}{2}$ capsicum, chopped finely
Leaves of 3 shallots, chopped
$\frac{1}{4}$ teaspoon turmeric
$\frac{1}{4}$ teaspoon cummin
Salt and pepper
$\frac{1}{4}$ teaspoon chilli powder (optional)
2 eggs, beaten
Water as required for mixing
1 cup cooking oil

Put prawns in a bowl, add rice flour, self-raising flour, cornflour, baking powder, semolina flour, besan flour, onion, ginger, capsicum, shallot leaves, turmeric, cummin, salt and pepper to taste, chilli powder (optional) and beaten eggs.
Mix well and add sufficient water to make a thick paste. Allow to stand for 15 minutes.
Heat cooking oil in a frying pan on moderate heat. Drop one tablespoon of batter at a time into the oil and fry until golden brown on both sides. Drain well and arrange on a plate.
Serve hot with tomato sauce or chilli sauce as a dip.

Yield: 20–24

INDIAN MIXTURE

250 g (8 oz) yellow lentils
Water
Cooking oil
Salt
125 g (4 oz) raw peanuts
125 g (4 oz) potato straws

Soak lentils in water overnight.
Wash, and drain thoroughly.
Heat cooking oil in a saucepan. Place lentils, a handful or two at a time, into a strainer, and lower into hot oil.
Deep fry lentils until golden brown, remove and drain thoroughly, and sprinkle with salt to taste. When lentils are cool, mix with peanuts and potato straws. Store in an air-tight jar.
Serve with drinks.

FISH BALLS

500 g (1 lb) jewfish *or* similar fish fillets
2 tablespoons cornflour
Thin slice ginger, pounded
2 shallots, chopped finely
Salt and pepper
½ cup cooking oil
Chilli sauce *or* tomato sauce

Wash and drain fish, remove any bones. Pound until smooth and soft, then put into a bowl.
Add cornflour, ginger, shallots, salt and pepper to taste. Mix well, then shape into small balls.
Heat oil in a frying pan on moderate heat, add fish balls, and fry until brown on all sides.
Drain well and arrange on a plate.
Serve hot with chilli sauce or tomato sauce as a dip.

Yield: 12–15

SAVOURY PRAWNS

500 g (1 lb) small cooked prawns, shelled
½ teaspoon chilli paste *or* 1 tablespoon chilli sauce
¼ teaspoon turmeric
Salt
¼ cup cooking oil
1 large onion, chopped finely
1 tablespoon lime juice
1 teaspoon sugar

Put prawns in a bowl, add chilli paste, turmeric and salt to taste and put aside.
Heat oil in a frying pan on moderate heat, add onion and fry until lightly browned.
Add seasoned prawns and fry for 10 minutes, stirring.
Add lime juice and sugar. Cook and stir for a further 5 minutes, then remove from heat.
Serve hot on toast or rice. Delicious with Coconut Rice (p. 71).

Serves 4–6

VEGETABLE AND POTATO FRITTERS
Bhajas

2 cups besan flour
½ cup self-raising flour
2 tablespoons cornflour
3 tablespoons rice flour
1 teaspoon baking powder
1 large potato, shredded
1 large carrot, shredded
1 large onion, chopped
¼ teaspoon chilli powder
¼ teaspoon cummin
¼ teaspoon turmeric
Salt
3 shallots, chopped finely
1 cup water (or more if
    needed)
1 teaspoon lemon juice
1½ cups cooking oil

In a mixing bowl, mix besan flour, self-raising flour, cornflour, rice flour, baking powder, potato, carrot, onion, chilli, cummin, turmeric, salt to taste, chopped shallots, water, lemon juice, and 1 tablespoon of the oil. Mix well to form a thick batter, and allow to stand for 5 minutes.

Heat remaining oil in a frying pan on moderate heat. Drop batter, 1 tablespoon at a time, into the oil, and fry fritters on both sides until golden brown.

Drain well and serve hot with chutneys, chilli sauce or tomato sauce.

Yield: 20

PRAWN AND PORK BALLS

500 g (1 lb) small cooked
    prawns, shelled and minced
250 g (½ lb) pork with fat,
    minced
¼ teaspoon sesame oil
1 small onion, minced
2 sprigs celery leaves, minced
2 shallots, minced
¼ teaspoon each turmeric,
    clove powder, cummin,
    cinnamon
2 cloves garlic, crushed *or* ½
    teaspoon garlic powder
1 tablespoon cornflour
2 tablespoons breadcrumbs
Salt and pepper
1 egg, beaten well
1 cup cooking oil

In a bowl, thoroughly mix all ingredients except cooking oil. Allow to stand for 5 minutes.

Shape mixture into small balls.

Heat oil in a frying pan on moderate heat. Drop meat balls, a few at a time, into the oil and deep fry until golden brown. Drain well and arrange on a plate.

Serve hot with chilli sauce or tomato sauce as a dip.

Yield: 15–20

FISH FRITTERS

500 g (1 lb) hake *or* kingfish fillets, cut into 15 mm ($\frac{1}{2}$ in) cubes
1 cup besan flour
3 tablespoons rice flour
1 tablespoon cornflour
1 tablespoon self-raising flour
$\frac{1}{2}$ teaspoon baking powder
1 fresh green chilli *or* $\frac{1}{2}$ capsicum, chopped finely
1 large onion, chopped finely
Thin slice fresh ginger, chopped finely
Leaves of 4 shallots, chopped
$\frac{1}{4}$ teaspoon pepper
$\frac{1}{4}$ teaspoon turmeric
1 egg, beaten well
Salt
1 cup water (or more if needed)
1 cup cooking oil

Put fish cubes in a bowl and add besan flour, rice flour, cornflour, self-raising flour, baking powder, chillies or capsicum, onion, ginger, shallot leaves, pepper, turmeric, egg, salt to taste.

Mix thoroughly and add water to make a thick batter. Allow to stand for 15 minutes.

Heat oil in a frying pan on moderate heat. Drop one tablespoon of the batter at a time into the pan and fry on both sides until golden brown. Drain well and arrange on a plate.

Serve hot with tomato sauce or chilli sauce as a dip.

Yield: 20–24

SPICY PRAWN FRITTERS

500 g (1 lb) small cooked prawns, shelled and chopped coarsely
1 cup plain flour
$\frac{1}{2}$ cup rice flour
1 teaspoon baking powder
Salt
$\frac{1}{2}$ teaspoon coriander *or* curry powder
$\frac{1}{2}$ teaspoon paprika (optional)
1 egg, beaten well
1 fresh green chilli, chopped (optional)
1 large onion, chopped
1 cup water
1 cup cooking oil

Put prawns into a bowl and add all other ingredients except cooking oil. Mix well to form a thick batter and allow to stand for 10 minutes.

Heat oil in a frying pan on moderate heat. Drop 1 tablespoon of batter at a time into the pan. Deep fry until golden brown on both sides. Drain well and arrange on a plate.

Serve hot with chilli sauce or tomato sauce as a dip.

Yield: 20–24

Hot Spicy Vegetables (p. 81) with Chapati (p. 20).
Overleaf: *left* — Pickled Pork (p. 66) with Puris (p. 24); *right* —Vegetable and Potato Fritters (p. 17), Fried Meat Balls (p. 19) and Savoury Prawns (p. 16).

CHEESE AND POTATO FRITTERS

1 cup self-raising flour
1 cup grated cheese
1 large onion, chopped
2 eggs, beaten well
1 teaspoon baking powder
Salt and pepper
1 teaspoon paprika
½ cup evaporated milk
2 cups cooking oil

In a bowl, mix self-raising flour, grated cheese, potatoes, beaten eggs, baking powder, salt and pepper to taste, paprika and milk. Mix well to make a thick batter and allow to stand for 5 minutes.

Heat oil in a frying pan on moderate heat. Drop batter, one tablespoon at a time, into the oil, and fry fritters on both sides until golden brown.

Drain well and serve hot with chilli sauce or chutneys.

Yield: 15–20

FRIED MEAT BALLS

500 g (1 lb) beef *or* pork, minced
2 tablespoons finely chopped onion
Thin slice ginger, chopped finely
Salt and pepper
2 tablespoons coriander *or* curry powder
1 egg, beaten
1 tablespoon worcestershire sauce
1 slice white bread, soaked in water and squeezed out
Leaves of 2 shallots, chopped finely
1 tablespoon breadcrumbs
¼ teaspoon cinnamon
¼ teaspoon clove powder
¼ teaspoon turmeric
1 cup cooking oil (or more if needed)

In a bowl, mix all ingredients except cooking oil thoroughly.

Shape mixture into balls about 25 mm (1 in) in diameter.

In a frying pan, heat oil and fry meat balls until brown on all sides, turning carefully without breaking. When cooked, drain well and serve hot or cold with Spicy Sauce (p. 96) or chilli or tomato sauce.

Serves 4–6

Minced Pork Balls with Yoghurt Sauce (p. 57).

BREAD

All Indian dishes, except desserts and sweets, are eaten with bread or rice — but bread and rice are not usually eaten together. There are several kinds of bread eaten in India; here I have given examples of the three main variations — Chapati, the flat, shallow-fried bread which is perhaps the best known, Puris, deep-fried, puffed-up and golden brown, and Paratha, shallow-fried and plain or stuffed with seasoned potato. All are best served as soon as possible after cooking, but can be kept for a short time by being wrapped in a clean, warm cloth and put in a warm place.

I have also included in this chapter a recipe for Dosa (rice flour and blackgram pancakes) and instructions for cooking Pappadums, wafer-thin lentil cakes which may be bought in packets and fried at home, to serve as a curry accompaniment or savoury.

CHAPATI

4 cups wholemeal flour
1 teaspoon baking powder
Salt
1 tablespoon ghee *or* butter
Water as required
Extra ghee or butter

In a bowl, mix together wholemeal flour, baking powder, and salt to taste. Rub in 1 tablespoon ghee or butter.

Add water, a little at a time, while kneading, to make a soft dough.

Continue rolling and kneading for 10 minutes, pressing and folding the dough, then cover with a wet cloth and allow to stand for 1 hour to rise.

For good results, knead **dough** again, then divide into pieces about the size cf a small egg, and shape these into round balls. Roll balls out into flat rounds about 100 mm (4 in) in diameter, and 3 mm ($\frac{1}{8}$ in) thick.

Heat a frying pan, smear with a little ghee or butter, and add one chapati at a time. Cook over medium heat.

When chapati is dry and bubbles appear, turn over and cook the other side until brown. Remove from heat and brush over a teaspoon of ghee or butter. Serve immediately with curry, vegetables, chutney or pickles.

Yield: 8–10

Note: Chapatis are best served immediately, but if made a little in advance, wrap in a napkin and keep in a warm place until serving time.

DOSA

3 cups rice flour
1 cup blackgram flour
Pinch bicarbonate of soda
2½ cups of water (or more if
   needed)
Salt
Cooking oil

In a bowl, mix rice flour, blackgram flour and soda with water to make a thick batter. Leave for 4 to 5 hours to rise.

Beat the mixture well. If the batter is thick add a little water and beat again until it is of pouring consistency. Add salt to taste.

Heat a griddle or frying pan on moderate heat and grease with a teaspoon of oil. Spread ½ a cup or a ladle full of batter thinly in pan. When bubbles appear on the surface, and underside is browned, turn pancake and cook for about 3 minutes. Remove like ordinary pancake.

Serve hot with Coconut Chutney (p. 93) or lentil curry (p. 84).

Yield: 15–16

PARATHA

6 cups plain flour
½ teaspoon bicarbonate of soda
Salt
½ teaspoon sugar
1 egg, beaten
4 tablespoons natural yoghurt
   or 1 cup milk
½ teaspoon ghee or butter
Warm water as required
Extra ghee or butter or oil for
   frying

In a bowl, mix flour, bicarbonate of soda and salt to taste, then add sugar, egg, yoghurt or milk.

Add warm water, a little at a time, and knead well to make a soft dough. Continue kneading until dough does not stick to fingers or sides of bowl. Rub ½ teaspoon of ghee or butter on the hand and continue kneading until dough is soft. (10 to 15 minutes). Cover with a wet cloth and allow to stand for 3 hours.

Divide dough into 8 or 10 equal parts and shape them into balls. Roll balls out into rounds about 80 mm (3 in) in diameter. Keep on a tray, covered with a tea towel.

Heat a frying pan or griddle, add 1 teaspoon of ghee or butter and fry paratha, one at a time, until light brown and puffed up. Add a little more ghee or butter to pan, turn and fry on other side. Remove when brown.

Serve hot with sugar or jam or with any curry. Delicious with Potato Curry (p. 85) and chutney.

Yield: 8–10

STUFFED PARATHA

Dough
500 g (1 lb) plain flour
2 tablespoons ghee *or* butter
Salt
1 cup water (or more if needed)

Stuffing
1 tablespoon cooking oil
500 g (1 lb) potatoes, boiled and mashed
1 onion, chopped finely
½ teaspoon paprika
¼ teaspoon garam masala
½ teaspoon coriander *or* curry powder
1 fresh green chilli, chopped (optional)
1 tablespoon lemon juice
Salt
1 tablespoon finely chopped shallot leaves
Extra ghee *or* butter for frying

In a bowl, mix flour, 2 tablespoons ghee or butter, salt and water to make a soft dough. Allow to stand for 1 hour, covered with a wet cloth to prevent drying.
Heat 1 tablespoon of oil in a pan, add onion and fry lightly.
Add mashed potatoes, paprika, garam masala, coriander, chilli (optional), lemon juice and salt to taste. Fry, stirring, for 5 minutes. Remove from heat and put aside.
Divide dough into equal parts, and shape into balls a little larger than an egg. Roll each ball into a flat, round shape, about 125 mm (5 in) in diameter.
Place a small quantity of the potato mixture on a round, and spread evenly with a spoon. Place another round on top, and roll gently. Press edges between fingers to seal. Repeat until dough and mixture has been used up.
Heat a frying pan, add 1 tablespoon ghee or butter and fry stuffed paratha, first browning one side, then the other.
Brush with a little more ghee or butter and remove from heat.
Serve hot with curry or chutney.

Serves 6

WHOLEMEAL PARATHA

4 cups wholemeal flour
1 teaspoon baking powder
1 teaspoon sugar
4 tablespoons ghee *or* butter
Salt
1 cup water (or more if needed)
Extra ghee *or* butter *or* oil for frying

In a bowl, mix the flour, baking powder, sugar, 4 tablespoons ghee, butter or oil and salt to taste.
Add water a little at a time (do not add too much water as dough will become sticky) and knead well to make a soft dough. Continue kneading, pressing and folding for 20 minutes, then cover with a wet cloth and leave to rise for 1 hour.
Knead again when ready to use. If dough is sticky, moisten fingers with little ghee, butter or oil. Dough should be kneaded thoroughly if good results are to be obtained.

(continued)

Divide the dough into 6 or 8 equal parts and shape them into balls.

Roll each ball into a flat, round shape about 125 mm (5 in) in diameter.

Spread round with little ghee, butter or oil and fold it into a ball, then roll again into a flat, round shape about 125 mm (5 in) in diameter.

Heat a frying pan over a slow flame, smear with a little ghee, butter or oil and add paratha. When lightly cooked and crisp on the underside, add little more ghee, butter or oil and turn. Fry until crisp and golden brown on both sides.

Serve immediately with curry or vegetables.

Yield: 8–10

PAPPADUMS

Pappadums
Cooking oil

Packets of pappadums may be bought at specialty shops and some supermarkets. They look like round wafers, but swell and increase in size when fried in hot oil.

Pour cooking oil into a frying pan to a depth of at least 25 mm (1 in). Heat the oil until it is smoking. If the oil is not hot enough, the pappadum will not swell sufficiently, and will be tough and oily.

Add one pappadum to the pan—it should immediately swell, curl and double its size. Quickly turn pappadum, using a fork or kitchen tongs, leave a second or two, and remove.

Repeat as many times as required, making sure that oil maintains correct temperature, especially if extra is added.

Serve as soon as possible after cooking. Pappadums go soft and limp quickly, but can be kept in an airtight tin for about 5 or 6 hours, once cool.

Note: Pappadums should not be browned, but ideally remain creamy white. This means that the cook must work very quickly in turning and removing them, and attempt to fry only one at a time.

PURIS

250 g (½ lb) wholemeal flour
250 g (½ lb) plain flour
1 teaspoon baking powder
¼ teaspoon cummin
Salt
1 tablespoon ghee *or* butter
1 cup cold water (or more if
    needed)
2 cups cooking oil *or* 1 cup
    cooking oil with 4
    tablespoons ghee or butter

In a bowl, mix both flours together with baking powder, then add cummin, salt to taste and 1 tablespoon ghee or butter. Work ghee through flour with fingers.

Add water to make a stiff dough and knead for 10 minutes. Allow to stand for 2 hours or more, covered with a wet cloth to prevent drying.

Knead again, and divide dough into even portions, about as big as a ping-pong ball. Roll into thin rounds about 125 mm (5 in) in diameter.

Heat oil in a frying pan. Drop one round at a time gently into the oil. When light brown in colour, turn to fry other side. When puri is light brown and puffed up, remove and drain.

Serve hot with Potato Curry (p. 85), any other curry or pickle, or for breakfast with jam.

Yield: 8–10

FISH

The following fish and prawn dishes are delicious served with rice and vegetables, or accompanying a meat curry. In most cases I have specified the ideal fish to be used in a recipe — but do not hesitate to try other kinds if these are not available. Look for firm-fleshed, white fish. In India, fish dishes are usually cooked with oil rather than ghee or butter.

You will find more prawn recipes in the Savouries chapter.

PRAWNS IN GARLIC AND CHILLI SAUCE

1 kg (2 lb) king prawns, shelled
3 cloves garlic, crushed
2 teaspoons sugar
1 chicken stock cube
1 teaspoon soy sauce
½ teaspoon sesame oil
2 tablespoons cornflour
Salt and pepper
5 tablespoons cooking oil
2 teaspoons oyster sauce (optional)
2 tablespoons water
1 tablespoon ginger wine
1 tablespoon chilli sauce
1 tablespoon tomato sauce
1 large onion, cubed
1 capsicum, cubed
2 shallots, chopped

Put prawns in a bowl and add garlic, sugar, chicken stock cube, soy sauce, sesame oil, 1 tablespoon of the cornflour, and salt and pepper to taste. Mix well and allow to stand for 10 minutes.

In a frying pan, heat 4 tablespoons of the oil, add prawns and fry for 5 minutes, then remove to a plate.

In a bowl, mix oyster sauce (optional), remaining 1 tablespoon cornflour, mixed to a paste with 2 tablespoons water, ginger wine, chilli sauce and tomato sauce. Mix well to form a paste, and put aside.

In a large pan, heat remaining 1 tablespoon oil, add onion cubes and fry for 2 minutes, then add capsicum and stir.

Add fried prawns to pan, then the mixed sauce paste. Stir gently. Continue to fry for 5 minutes until the sauce is thick.

Remove from heat and sprinkle with chopped shallots.

Transfer to a flat plate and serve hot with rice.

Serves 6–8

PRAWN AND CUCUMBER CURRY

750 g (1½ lb) large prawns,
    shelled, but with tails
    intact
½ teaspoon paprika *or* chilli
    powder (optional)
1 tablespoon curry powder
Pinch turmeric
Thin slice ginger, cut into
    strips
1 clove garlic, crushed
Salt
3 tablespoons cooking oil
1 large onion, sliced finely
1 cup canned coconut milk
    or 30 g (2 oz) coconut
    cream mixed with 1 cup
    of water
1 cucumber, peeled, seeded
    and cubed
2 fresh green chillies, halved
1 tablespoon vinegar

In a bowl, mix prawns, paprika or chilli powder
(optional), curry powder, turmeric, ginger, garlic
and salt to taste and allow to stand for 5 minutes.
Heat oil in a frying pan, fry onion until golden
brown.
Add seasoned prawns and fry, stirring for 10
minutes.
Add cream of coconut and cucumber, mix well
and bring to the boil.
Add green chillies and vinegar, boil for 2 seconds
only, stir and remove from heat.
Serve hot with rice or bread.

Serves 4

PRAWNS IN COCONUT

500 g (1 lb) medium
    prawns, shelled
1 teaspoon vinegar
Salt and pepper
Pinch turmeric
3 tablespoons cooking oil
¼ teaspoon mustard seed
1 teaspoon uncooked rice
1 small onion, chopped
1 clove garlic, chopped
Thin slice ginger, chopped
2 fresh green chillies, halved
    or ½ capsicum, chopped
2 curry leaves
4 tablespoons desiccated
    coconut

Put prawns in a bowl, add vinegar, salt and pepper
to taste, and turmeric. Mix well and allow to stand
for 15 minutes.
In a frying pan, heat cooking oil, add mustard seed
and fry for 2 seconds only, then add rice and fry
until it bubbles.
Add onions and fry until golden brown. Add
garlic and ginger and fry for 2 minutes, stirring.
Add seasoned prawns, fry for 10 minutes, stirring
constantly, then add chillies, curry leaves and
desiccated coconut. Continue to cook and stir for 5
minutes and remove from heat.
Serve with fluffy rice and vegetables.

Serves 4

PRAWNS, PORK AND BAMBOO SHOOTS FRIED IN SAUCE

250 g ($\frac{1}{2}$ lb) medium prawns, shelled

250 g ($\frac{1}{2}$ lb) leg of pork, cut into 25 mm (1 in) cubes

Salt and pepper

$\frac{1}{4}$ teaspoon monosodium glutamate (optional)

$\frac{1}{2}$ teaspoon sugar

2 chicken stock cubes

1 teaspoon soy sauce

$\frac{1}{2}$ teaspoon sesame oil

2 tablespoons cooking oil

1 tablespoon worcestershire sauce

3 tablespoons water

1 teaspoon black bean sauce

2 tablespoons cornflour

185 g (6 oz) bamboo shoots, cubed

1 capsicum, cut into squares

1 cucumber, peeled, seeded and cubed

Garnish: 1 stalk celery, cubed
   2 tablespoons green peas, cooked

In a bowl, mix prawns, pork cubes, salt and pepper to taste, monosodium glutamate (optional), sugar, chicken stock cubes, soy sauce and sesame oil and allow to stand for 5 minutes. Remove pork to another bowl.

In a frying pan, heat oil, add seasoned prawns and fry for 5 minutes, stirring gently all the time. Remove prawns and put aside.

Add seasoned pork to pan and fry on all sides until cooked. Remove pork and put aside. Leave the remaining oil in the pan for later use.

In a bowl, mix worcestershire sauce, water, black bean sauce and cornflour, to form a paste.

Reheat oil in which prawns and pork were cooked and add sauce mixture, bamboo shoots, capsicum squares and cucumber cubes. Mix well, bring to the boil, and boil until sauce thickens.

Reduce heat and add fried prawns and pork. Mix well and remove to a serving dish.

Garnish with celery cubes and cooked peas.

Serves 4

PRAWNS IN SPICY CHILLI SAUCE

1 kg (2 lb) large prawns,
  shelled, but with tails
  intact
Salt and pepper
½ teaspoon vinegar
2 teaspoons worcestershire
  sauce
4 cloves garlic, crushed
Thin slice ginger, pounded
½ teaspoon ginger wine
1 teaspoon Maggi seasoning
2 tablespoons chilli sauce
1 tablespoon tomato sauce
1 tablespoon cornflour
  mixed with 2 tablespoons
  water
4 tablespoons cooking oil
1 large onion, cubed
½ capsicum, cubed

Put prawns in a bowl, add salt and pepper to taste, vinegar, worcestershire sauce, garlic, ginger, ginger wine, and Maggi seasoning. Mix well and allow to stand for 10 minutes.
In another bowl, mix chilli sauce, tomato sauce, and cornflour and water to form a paste, and put aside.
In a frying pan, heat oil, fry onion and capsicum for 3 minutes, remove and put aside.
In the same oil fry seasoned prawns for 5 minutes, then add the chilli paste and reduce heat. Cook for 5 minutes, stirring to prevent burning.
When oil rises, add fried onions and capsicum, mix again and remove to a flat plate.
Serve with fried rice.

Serves 6

PRAWNS AND CAULIFLOWER WITH CRABMEAT

500 g (1 lb) king prawns,
  shelled and cut into
  desired pieces
½ teaspoon sugar
Salt and pepper
1 clove garlic, crushed
½ teaspoon sesame oil
½ teaspoon monosodium
  glutamate
1 chicken stock cube
3 tablespoons cooking oil
250 g (½ lb) cauliflower,
  broken into large pieces
2 tablespoons frozen green
  peas
60 g (4 oz) canned crabmeat
1 egg, beaten well
Garnish: 2 celery leaves *or*
  sprigs coriander, chopped

Put prawns in a bowl, add sugar, salt and pepper to taste, garlic, sesame oil, monosodium glutamate and chicken stock cube and allow to stand for 10 minutes.
In a frying pan, heat cooking oil, add prawns and fry for 5 minutes, then add cauliflower pieces and green peas and fry for 3 minutes.
Add crabmeat and beaten egg. Continue to fry, stirring constantly, until mixture is dry and egg is well cooked, then remove from heat.
Garnish with chopped celery and serve with rice.

Serves 4–6

FISH CURRY WITH AUBERGINE AND TOMATO

2 tablespoons cooking oil
¼ teaspoon mustard seed
1 large onion, chopped
    finely
Thin slice ginger, shredded
1 clove garlic, sliced
250 g (½ lb) aubergine (egg-
    plant) *or* okra, peeled and
    cut into long pieces or
    quarters and soaked in
    water
Pinch turmeric
¼ teaspoon cummin
¼ teaspoon aniseed
Pinch nutmeg
Salt and pepper
1 fresh green chilli, sliced
    (optional)
3 curry leaves
2 tablespoons coriander *or*
    curry powder
1½ cups water
1 teaspoon vinegar
2 ripe tomatoes, quartered
750 g (1½ lb) fillets of
    kingfish or similar, cut
    into serving pieces
2 tablespoons canned
    coconut milk *or* 15 g
    (½ oz) coconut cream mixed
    with 2 tablespoons water
1 tablespoon lemon juice

Heat oil in a large saucepan, add mustard seed, fry for 2 seconds only, then add onions and fry until golden brown.

Reduce heat to moderate and add ginger, garlic, aubergine, turmeric, cummin, aniseed, nutmeg, salt and pepper to taste, chilli (optional), curry leaves, coriander and water. Stir gently, add vinegar and boil for 5 minutes, covered.

Add tomatoes, fish and coconut milk. Stir gently. Bring back to the boil, reduce heat, and allow to simmer for 15 minutes.

Add lemon juice, bring to boil and remove from heat. (If more gravy is needed, add ½ cup of water with the lemon juice.) Serve hot with rice and salad.

Serves 6

FISH HEAD CURRY

1 large jewfish *or* kingfish
head (about 1 kg [2 lb]),
cut into halves or quarters
2 tablespoons coriander *or*
curry powder
½ teaspoon chilli powder
(optional)
Pinch turmeric
Pinch cummin
1 cup tamarind juice
Salt
2 curry leaves
3 tablespoons cooking oil
1 large onion, sliced finely
Thin slice ginger, sliced
finely
4 ripe tomatoes, quartered
60 g (2 oz) coconut cream
mixed with ½ cup water

Put the fish head pieces in a bowl, mix with coriander, chilli powder (optional), turmeric, cummin, tamarind juice, salt to taste and 2 curry leaves and put aside.

Heat oil in a saucepan, add onion and fry until golden brown.

Add ginger and fry for 2 minutes, then add seasoned fish head pieces and marinade. Cover pan, bring to the boil, reduce heat and simmer for 15 minutes.

Remove lid, add tomatoes and cream of coconut, stir, then bring to boil and remove from heat.

Serve hot with rice and vegetables.

Serves 4

HOT FISH PICKLE
Achar

1 kg (2 lb) kingfish *or*
jewfish fillets *or* 500 g (1 lb)
dried fish fillets, cubed
Salt
¼ teaspoon turmeric
1¼ cup cooking oil
1 teaspoon mustard seed,
pounded coarsely
¼ teaspoon fenugreek seed
(optional)
¼ teaspoon pepper
3 tablespoons chilli powder
or paprika
5 mm (¼ in) slice ginger,
chopped finely
3 cloves garlic, chopped
finely
½ cup vinegar, boiled and
cooled

Put fish cubes in a bowl, add salt to taste and turmeric powder, mix well.

Heat oil in a frying pan and fry fish cubes until brown, then remove from pan and put aside.

In the remaining oil, fry mustard seed for 2 seconds only, then reduce heat to low and add fenugreek seed (optional), pepper, chilli powder, ginger and garlic. Mix well, increase heat to moderate, and fry for 5 minutes.

Add fried fish, then boiled vinegar, stir gently and simmer until oil rises, then remove from heat.

When cool, put into a sterilised, air-tight bottle, and allow to stand for 2 days before using.

Note: This fish pickle may be kept for weeks, if desired. It is usually used as a side dish.

FISH WITH FRESH CHILLIES AND TAMARIND

$\frac{1}{2}$ tablespoon chilli powder
$2\frac{1}{2}$ tablespoons coriander *or*
   curry powder
3 curry leaves
Salt
1 tablespoon tamarind paste
   or 6 tablespoons tamarind
   water
Pinch turmeric
$\frac{1}{4}$ teaspoon black pepper
1 cup water
3 tablespoons cooking oil
1 large onion, sliced finely
Thin slice ginger, shredded
6 fresh green chillies, halved
1 kg (2 lb) whole or filleted
   kingfish *or* Spanish
   mackerel *or* pomfret, with
   bones, cut into 20 mm
   ($\frac{3}{4}$ in) thick slices
1 teaspoon vinegar
2 tablespoons evaporated
   milk
1 teaspoon peanut oil

In a bowl, mix chilli powder, coriander, curry leaves, salt to taste, tamarind paste, turmeric, black pepper and water to form a watery paste and put aside.

Heat cooking oil in a saucepan, add onion and fry until golden brown.

Add ginger and chillies, fry for 2 seconds only, then add the mixed paste and fry, stirring, for 5 minutes.

Reduce heat to low, add fish and vinegar, stir well, cover, and simmer until fish is cooked.

Remove lid and add evaporated milk and peanut oil. Mix well. Bring to the boil, remove from heat and serve.

Serve with fluffy rice.

Serves 4–6

HOT FISH CURRY

2 tablespoons chilli paste *or*
    1½ tablespoons chilli
    powder
1½ tablespoons coriander *or*
    curry powder
¼ teaspoon turmeric
¼ teaspoon nutmeg
¼ teaspoon black pepper
1 cup water
2 curry leaves
Salt
1 tablespoon tamarind paste
    or ½ cup tamarind water
3½ tablespoons cooking oil
¼ teaspoon mustard seed
1 small onion, sliced *or*
    chopped finely
2 fresh green chillies, halved
Thin slice ginger, shredded
    finely
750 g (1½ lb) hake *or* any
    other fleshy fish, cut into
    25 mm (1 in) thick slices
    or prawns
¼ teaspoon roasted fenugreek
    seed, pounded into
    powder

In a small bowl, mix chilli paste, coriander, turmeric, nutmeg, black pepper, water, curry leaves, salt to taste and tamarind paste and put aside.

Heat oil in a large saucepan, add mustard seed, fry for 2 seconds only, then add onions and fry until golden brown.

Add garlic, chillies, ginger and the mixed spices, stir and boil for 5 minutes.

Add fish slices and roasted fenugreek powder and boil slowly until gravy thickens and fish is cooked. Serve hot with rice or bread and vegetables.

Serves 4

HOT FISH CURRY MADRAS STYLE

4 tablespoons chilli powder
1 tablespoon coriander *or*
    curry powder
¼ teaspoon white pepper
¼ teaspoon turmeric
¼ teaspoon fenugreek seed,
    pounded into powder
3 tablespoons cooking oil
1 large onion, sliced finely

In a large saucepan, mix chilli powder, coriander, white pepper, turmeric and fenugreek powder and put aside.

In a frying pan, heat oil, add onion, and fry until golden brown. Add ginger and garlic and fry for 2 minutes.

Reduce heat, add tamarind juice and salt to taste and mix well. Pour slowly into the spice mixture in the saucepan. Bring to the boil and boil for 10

(continued)

(continued)

Thin slice ginger, chopped
  finely
1 clove garlic, minced
1 cup tamarind juice
Salt
1 kg (2 lb) whole or filleted
  jewfish *or* kingfish *or*
  hake, cut into serving
  pieces
1 teaspoon peanut oil

minutes, then add fish pieces and stir gently. Boil
gently until fish is cooked and gravy thickens.
Remove from heat, add 1 teaspoon peanut oil,
return to heat and bring to the boil.
Remove from heat and serve with rice and
vegetables.

Serves 4–6

Note: This curry will have a better flavour if
cooked the day before and warmed before serving.

FISH CAKES

750 g (1½ lb) kingfish *or*
  jewfish fillets
1¼ cups cooking oil
1 large onion, chopped
  finely
1 fresh green chilli *or* ½
  capsicum, chopped finely
Thin slice fresh ginger,
  chopped finely
3 sprigs coriander, chopped
  finely
Leaves of 3 shallots, chopped
  finely
¼ teaspoon pepper
1 teaspoon vinegar
¼ teaspoon cummin
¼ teaspoon turmeric
Salt
4 medium potatoes, peeled,
  boiled and mashed
1 egg, beaten well
½ cup breadcrumbs
Garnish: 1 large onion, cut
  into 15 mm (½ in) slices
  and fried until brown *or*
  left raw

Put fish fillets in saucepan with cold water to cover.
Cover pan, bring to the boil, reduce heat and
simmer until fish is cooked. Remove fish and flake,
removing bones if any, and leave in a large bowl.
Heat 1 tablespoon of the oil in a frying pan, add
onions and fry until lightly browned.
Add chilli and ginger and fry for 5 minutes, then
pour contents of pan into fish.
Add coriander leaves, shallot leaves, pepper,
vinegar, cummin, turmeric, salt to taste and
mashed potatoes to the bowl. Mix well with fish
flakes.
Shape mixture into balls about the size of an egg or
into any desired shape and place on a plate.
Dip each ball into the beaten egg, then roll in the
breadcrumbs.
Heat cooking oil in a frying pan, drop 3 or 4 cutlets
at a time into the oil, fry on both sides until golden
brown, then remove and drain.
Arrange fish cakes on a flat platter and garnish with
raw or fried onion rings.
Serve with Yellow Rice (p. 72) or as a savoury.

Serves 6–8

FISH CURRY

Salt and pepper
2½ teaspoons vinegar
2½ tablespoons coriander *or*
   curry powder
¼ teaspoon turmeric
¼ teaspoon nutmeg
¼ cup water
3 tablespoons cooking oil
1 large onion, sliced finely
Thin slice ginger, shredded
2 fresh green chillies *or* 1
   capsicum, sliced
2 dry red chillies, broken
   into pieces (optional)
1 kg (2 lb) kingfish *or* other
   white fish fillets, cut into
   serving pieces
1½ cups canned coconut milk
   or 125 g (4 oz) coconut
   cream mixed with 1½ cups
   water *or* 1½ cups
   evaporated milk
1 tomato, quartered
1 tablespoon lemon juice

In a small bowl, mix salt and pepper to taste, vinegar, coriander, turmeric, nutmeg and water to form a paste, and put aside.

Heat 2 tablespoons of cooking oil in a frying pan, add onion and fry until golden brown.

Add ginger, green chillies and red chillies (optional). Fry for 2 minutes.

Add the mixed spice paste, fry for 10 seconds only, then pour contents of pan into a saucepan.

Add fish pieces, mix gently, cover and cook for 10 minutes.

Remove lid of pan, reduce heat, and add coconut cream. Stir well, then add tomato and lemon juice. Stir again and bring to the boil.

Remove from heat and serve with rice and vegetables.

Serves 4–6

FISH ROE WITH COCONUT

250 g (½ lb) fresh fish roe,
   mashed
Salt and pepper
Pinch turmeric
3 tablespoons cooking oil
1 small onion, minced
1 fresh green chilli *or* ½
   capsicum, minced
Thin slice of ginger, minced
3 tablespoons desiccated
   coconut
2 eggs, beaten well

Put fish roe in a bowl, add salt and pepper to taste and turmeric, mix well and put aside.

Heat oil in a frying pan, add onions and fry until lightly browned.

Add chilli, ginger and the seasoned fish roe and fry for 2 minutes, stirring.

Add desiccated coconut and beaten eggs and continue frying, stirring continuously, until eggs are well cooked.

Remove from heat and serve hot with rice or on toast.

Serves 4

Kashmir Chilli Chicken in Tomatoes (p. 38) with
Cucumber and Pineapple Salad (p. 88).

COCONUT MILK CURRY
Sothi

4 cups canned coconut milk
   or 315 g (10 oz) coconut
   cream mixed with 4 cups
   water
250 g ($\frac{1}{2}$ lb) hake *or* jewfish
   fillets, cut into 50 mm
   (2 in) squares
Salt
$\frac{1}{2}$ teaspoon turmeric
2 curry leaves
1 tablespoon cooking oil
$\frac{1}{2}$ teaspoon mustard seed
1 large onion, sliced finely
3 fresh green chillies,
   coarsely sliced
1 tablespoon lime juice (or to
   taste)

In a large saucepan, mix coconut milk, fish, salt to taste, turmeric and curry leaves and put aside.

In a frying pan, heat cooking oil add mustard seed and fry for 2 seconds only, then add onion and fry until golden brown.

Add chillies, remove pan from heat and pour all the fried ingredients into the saucepan.

Mix gently, bring to the boil and boil slowly until fish is cooked.

Add lime juice, stir, bring to boil and remove from heat.

Serve with white rice and any dry curries. Sothi curry is usually poured over the white rice.

Serves 6–8

Persian Chicken Roast (p. 40) with Rice with Red Lentils
(p. 73) and Yoghurt with Cucumber (p. 89).

CHICKEN AND DUCK

The following recipes may be used for partridge, pheasant and quail, as well as for chicken and duck, if desired—game birds are enjoyed in many parts of India. You will find more chicken recipes in other chapters—notably the Meat section, where chicken may often be used as an alternative to beef, lamb or pork. Consult the index for the full range of chicken recipes.

Poultry may be baked, whole or in pieces, barbecued, fried, stewed and steamed, and you will find the whole range of cooking methods here. For many of the dishes calling for the chicken to be jointed, you may find it a good idea to buy chicken pieces rather than a whole bird—this way you can ensure that everyone has the part of the chicken he or she likes best, and save time as well! Be sure, however, that the chicken pieces are of high quality—not too large and tough. Frozen chickens are convenient, readily available and less expensive than fresh, but they are in general inferior in flavour. For the baked and fried chicken dishes, particularly, a fresh chicken will give a much better result, so it is worth going to the trouble and spending a little extra to secure one.

MILD CHICKEN CURRY

Salt
1 teaspoon paprika
Thin slice ginger, pounded
¼ teaspoon clove powder
¼ teaspoon cinnamon
1 chicken, cut into serving
  pieces
½ cup cooking oil
1 large onion, sliced
400 ml (14½ fl oz) can
  tomato juice
½ cup water
2 ripe tomatoes, chopped
2 tablespoons coriander *or*
  curry powder (optional)
1 teaspoon lemon juice
  (optional)

In a large bowl mix salt, paprika, ginger, clove powder, and cinnamon.

Add chicken pieces to spice mixture, mix well to cover on all sides and put aside.

Heat oil in a saucepan, add onion and fry until golden brown, then add seasoned chicken, and stir over heat for 5 minutes.

Add tomato juice, water, tomatoes, coriander (optional), and lemon juice (optional) to pan. Bring mixture to the boil, then reduce heat and simmer until chicken is tender and sauce is thick. Remove from heat and serve with rice or bread.

Serves 4–6

CHICKEN BAKED IN CURRY SAUCE

2½ tablespoons coriander *or* curry powder
1 teaspoon paprika
½ teaspoon each cummin, aniseed, turmeric, pepper
4 candlenuts, pounded to a paste
15 mm (½ in) cube shrimp paste
1 stalk lemon grass (optional)
1 teaspoon sugar
1 teaspoon vinegar
1 slice galangal, grated (optional)
60 g (2 oz) coconut cream mixed with 1 cup water
2 tablespoons tamarind juice *or* 1 teaspoon tamarind paste
Salt
1 chicken, cut into serving pieces
3 tablespoons cooking oil
3 tablespoons melted butter
1 large onion, chopped finely
1 capsicum, cut into thick rings
Garnish: 1 onion, cut into 15 mm (½ in) slices and fried golden brown
1 tomato, cut into 15 mm (½ in) slices
1 cucumber, peeled and sliced
2 celery leaves, chopped
Leaves of 2 shallots, cut into 15 mm (½ in) lengths

In a bowl, mix coriander, paprika, cummin, aniseed, turmeric, pepper, pounded candlenuts, shrimp paste, lemon grass (optional), sugar, vinegar, galangal (optional), coconut cream mixture, tamarind juice and salt to taste.

In a frying pan, heat cooking oil and fry onions until golden brown.

Add the mixed paste from the bowl to the pan, mix well, and fry gently for 15 minutes, stirring constantly to prevent burning. Remove pan from heat and put aside.

Place chicken pieces in a baking dish and rub all over with the fried ingredients. Pour over melted butter. Bake in a moderate oven (175°C, 350°F), turning once or twice, until chicken is cooked and brown and gravy thickens. Remove from oven and garnish with fried onion.

To serve, pile chicken pieces and onion on a platter, place tomato and cucumber around the edge, and sprinkle celery and shallot leaves over all.

Serve hot with rice or bread.

Serves 4–6.

CHICKEN IN TOMATO

1 chicken, cut into serving
  pieces
Salt and pepper
2 teaspoons paprika
25 mm (1 in) piece fresh
  ginger, pounded
1 clove garlic, pounded
4 tablespoons cooking oil (or
  more if needed)
2 onions, sliced finely
3 tomatoes, diced
$\frac{1}{4}$ teaspoon cinnamon
$\frac{1}{4}$ teaspoon clove powder
Pinch turmeric
$\frac{3}{4}$ cup water
4 tablespoons tomato paste

In a large bowl mix salt, pepper, paprika, pounded ginger and garlic.

Add chicken pieces to spice mixture, mix well and allow to stand for 10 minutes.

Heat oil in frying pan, add onions and fry until golden brown, then add tomatoes and fry gently until soft.

Add seasoned chicken pieces to pan, then add cinnamon, clove powder and turmeric. Mix well. Cook for 15 minutes, stirring constantly.

Add water and tomato paste. Bring to boil, then reduce heat and simmer until chicken is tender, gravy begins to thicken and oil rises to the top. Remove from heat and serve with rice or bread.

Serves 4–6

KASHMIR CHILLI CHICKEN IN TOMATOES

6 tablespoons cooking oil
3 large onions, chopped
2 cloves garlic, crushed
Thin slice ginger, pounded
3 ripe tomatoes, chopped
  finely
2 tablespoons tomato puree
2 teaspoons chilli powder
2 tablespoons coriander *or*
  curry powder
$\frac{1}{4}$ teaspoon each cummin,
  aniseed, turmeric,
  clove powder, cinnamon,
  cardamom powder,
  pepper
1 chicken, cut into serving
  pieces
Salt
1 cup water
1 teaspoon vinegar
Lemon juice

Heat oil in a frying pan, add onions and fry until golden brown.

Add garlic, ginger, tomatoes, tomato puree, chilli powder, coriander, cummin, aniseed, turmeric, clove powder, cinnamon, cardamom powder and pepper. Fry gently for 15 minutes, stirring often to prevent burning.

Add chicken, salt to taste and water to pan, mix well and boil for 15 minutes, then add vinegar and lemon juice. Cook until chicken is tender, water has been absorbed and oil rises to the top.

Pour into a dish and serve hot with rice or bread and Cucumber and Pineapple Salad (p. 88).

Serves 4–6

CHICKEN IN SPICY SAUCE

1 chicken, cut into serving
  pieces
Salt and pepper
1 cup water
2 tablespoons cooking oil
1 large onion, chopped
5 mm ($\frac{1}{4}$ in) slice ginger,
  shredded finely
$\frac{1}{4}$ teaspoon cinnamon
1 tablespoon red wine *or*
  sherry
1 tablespoon worcestershire
  sauce
$\frac{1}{2}$ teaspoon thick soy sauce
1 capsicum, finely sliced
2 tablespoons tomato sauce
Garnish: leaves of 2 shallots,
  chopped

Rub salt and pepper on chicken pieces and place in a saucepan with the water. Bring to the boil, reduce heat and simmer gently, covered, until chicken is tender. Remove chicken and put aside. Heat oil in a pan, add onions and fry until lightly browned.

Reduce heat and add ginger, cooked chicken, cinnamon, red wine or sherry, worcestershire sauce, soy sauce, sliced capsicum and tomato sauce, stirring constantly to prevent burning.

Cook for 5 minutes, stirring all the time, and remove.

Garnish with chopped shallot leaves and serve with rice.

Serves 4–6

Note: A ready-cooked chicken may be used, if desired. Merely cut into serving pieces and add to the onions with the other ingredients.

FRIED CHICKEN WINGS

12 chicken wings, cut in half
  at the joints
4 cloves garlic, crushed
2 chicken stock cubes, made
  into a paste with 1
  tablespoon water
1 tablespoon cornflour
1 tablespoon soy sauce
$\frac{1}{2}$ teaspoon sesame oil
2 teaspoons sugar
4 tablespoons breadcrumbs
$1\frac{1}{4}$ cups cooking oil
Salt and pepper
Garnish: 1 sprig celery
  leaves, chopped
  1 red chilli, quartered
  1 cucumber, sliced

In a large bowl, mix garlic, chicken stock cubes, cornflour, soy sauce, sesame oil, sugar, breadcrumbs, 1 tablespoon of the cooking oil and salt and pepper.

Add chicken wings, mix thoroughly and allow to stand for 15 minutes.

Heat oil in frying pan and fry marinated chicken wings till golden brown, adding extra oil if necessary. Remove and drain.

Pile chicken wings on platter and garnish with chopped celery leaves, sliced cucumber and cut chillies.

Serve with Fried Rice (p. 70) and chilli sauce.

Serves 4

PERSIAN CHICKEN ROAST

3 tablespoons cooking oil
2 large onions, chopped
   finely
5 mm ($\frac{1}{4}$ in) slice ginger,
   pounded
2 cloves garlic, pounded
Salt and pepper
1 tablespoon vinegar
$\frac{1}{4}$ teaspoon cinnamon
$\frac{1}{4}$ teaspoon clove powder
$\frac{1}{4}$ teaspoon turmeric
2 tablespoons tomato paste
1 tablespoon honey
125 g (4 oz) coconut cream
   mixed with 1 cup water
   or 1 cup evaporated milk
1 chicken, cut into serving
   pieces *or* left whole
1 tablespoon lemon juice
1 tablespoon melted butter
Garnish: 1 large onion, cut
   into 15 mm ($\frac{1}{2}$ in) slices
   and fried golden brown
   1 cup cooked green peas

Heat oil in a pan and fry onions gently for 2 minutes. Add ginger and garlic and fry until just turning brown.

Place onion, ginger and garlic in a large bowl and add salt and pepper, vinegar, cinnamon, clove powder, turmeric, tomato paste, honey and coconut cream. Mix well.

Add chicken pieces to sauce and mix well until all pieces are coated.

Place chicken in a baking dish and bake in a moderate oven (175°C, 350°F), basting occasionally with pan juices and extra cooking oil, until well cooked and golden brown.

When cooked, sprinkle over lemon juice and brush on melted butter. Return to oven for 5 minutes. Remove and arrange on platter.

Garnish with fried onion rings and green peas, and serve.

Serves 4–6

CHICKEN BREASTS IN BREADCRUMBS

6 chicken breasts, boned and
   cut into thin slices
2 cloves garlic, crushed
$\frac{1}{2}$ teaspoon sesame oil
1 teaspoon sugar
$\frac{1}{2}$ teaspoon worcestershire
   sauce
Salt and pepper
3 cups breadcrumbs
1 cup cooking oil (or more
   if needed)

In a large bowl mix crushed garlic, sesame oil, sugar, worcestershire sauce and salt and pepper to taste.

Add chicken pieces, mix well, and allow to stand for 15 minutes.

Roll chicken pieces in breadcrumbs. Pat crumbs firmly on to chicken skin.

Heat oil in a pan and drop the crumbed slices in, 2 or 3 at a time. Fry until golden brown, drain, and place on a warmed, flat plate. Add extra oil to pan, as needed, as frying continues.

Serve with bread or rice, and salad.

Serves 6

FRIED CHICKEN LEGS WITH TOMATO SAUCE

12 chicken legs
2 eggs, beaten
Salt and pepper
3 tablespoons water
3½ tablespoons cornflour
2 tablespoons self-raising
   flour
1 teaspoon sugar
1¼ cups cooking oil
Sauce:
2 chicken stock cubes
1 tablespoon vinegar
1 tablespoon sugar
4 tablespoons tomato sauce
½ tablespoon soy sauce
Salt
2 large onions, cut into
   squares
1 red capsicum, cut into
   squares
1 carrot, sliced and parboiled
Garnish: 2 spring onion
   leaves, cut into 25 mm
   (1 in) pieces
   1 onion, sliced and fried
    golden brown
   ½ cup pineapple cubes,
    fresh or tinned
   6 lettuce leaves

Clean chicken legs and dry well.

In a bowl, mix beaten eggs, salt, pepper, and 1 tablespoon water. Mix 2 tablespoons cornflour, self-raising flour and 1 teaspoon sugar together on a plate.

Take chicken legs one by one and dip into egg mixture, then roll in flour mixture, and set aside. Put all but 2 tablespoons of oil into frying pan and heat. Fry chicken legs, a few at a time, until cooked and well browned. Remove, drain well, and keep warm.

In a bowl, mix remaining 2 tablespoons water, chicken stock cubes, vinegar, sugar, remaining 1½ tablespoons cornflour, tomato sauce, soy sauce and salt. Mix thoroughly to make a paste.

Heat 2 tablespoons cooking oil in a pan. Fry onions, capsicum and carrots for 2 minutes, then add the mixed sauce paste and boil gently until thickened.

Place fried chicken legs on a bed of lettuce on a platter, pour sauce over and sprinkle with chopped spring onion leaves and fried onion. Decorate with cubed pineapple.

Serves 4–6

SPICY CHICKEN AND RICE PORRIDGE

2 cups rice, washed and
   drained
2 chicken stock cubes, mixed
   with a little water to
   make a paste
Salt and pepper
Pinch turmeric
6 cups water
1 tablespoon peanut oil
1 large onion, chopped
   finely
1 large, ripe tomato, minced
1 tablespoon tomato paste
$\frac{1}{4}$ teaspoon cinnamon
1 medium carrot, shredded
Few cabbage leaves,
   shredded
1 teaspoon ginger wine
2 chicken breasts, boiled and
   shredded
Few celery leaves, chopped

Put rice in pot, add chicken stock, salt and pepper, turmeric and water and boil gently for 1 hour.

In a pan heat peanut oil, fry onion until golden brown then add tomato, tomato paste, cinnamon, carrot and cabbage. Mix well and fry for 2 minutes.

Pour vegetable mixture into the boiled rice, add ginger wine, then shredded chicken breasts. Mix well.

Reduce heat and keep mixture simmering until rice is soft, stirring occasionally and adding water if necessary to prevent sticking.

When mixture resembles thick porridge, add chopped celery leaves and serve with Ginger Sauce (p.97).

Serves 8

CHICKEN IN MILK SAUCE

12 chicken pieces
2 cups water
Salt and pepper
$1\frac{1}{2}$ teaspoons sugar
1 teaspoon sesame oil
Pinch monosodium
   glutamate
$1\frac{1}{4}$ cups cooking oil
3 tablespoons evaporated
   milk
1 egg white
Garnish: few lettuce leaves

Put chicken pieces in saucepan with water and steam over moderate heat until cooked.

Remove chicken pieces, reserving stock. Wash chicken pieces with hot water.

Strain stock into a bowl and add salt and pepper to taste, sugar, sesame oil and monosodium glutamate. Mix well. Add chicken pieces to stock mixture and mix well. Allow chicken to marinate for 30 minutes. Remove, reserving marinade.

Heat all but 2 tablespoons of the cooking oil in a frying pan, add chicken pieces. Fry until golden brown, but not too crispy, remove to a platter and keep warm.

(continued)

Add evaporated milk and egg white to the left-over sauce in the marinating dish, and mix well. In another pan, heat remaining 2 tablespoons cooking oil. Slowly add the milk sauce, bring to the boil and simmer for 5 minutes over a low heat until the sauce thickens. Remove from heat and pour over chicken pieces.

Place lettuce leaves around chicken pieces, and serve.

Serves 6

CHICKEN AND POTATO CURRY

1 chicken, cut into serving
    pieces
3 tablespoons coriander *or*
    curry powder
1 teaspoon paprika (optional)
$\frac{1}{4}$ teaspoon each white
    pepper, turmeric, aniseed,
    cummin, cinnamon, clove
    powder, cardamom
    powder
1 teaspoon vinegar
Salt
$\frac{1}{4}$ cup water
3 tablespoons cooking oil
$\frac{1}{2}$ teaspoon mustard seed
1 large onion, chopped
    finely
1 clove garlic, crushed
Thin slice ginger, shredded
3 large potatoes, quartered
125 g (4 oz) coconut cream
    mixed with 1 cup water
    or $\frac{1}{2}$ cup evaporated milk
    mixed with $\frac{1}{2}$ cup water
1 teaspoon lemon juice

In a large saucepan mix coriander, paprika (optional), white pepper, turmeric, aniseed, cummin, cinnamon, clove powder, cardamom powder, vinegar, salt to taste and water. Add chicken pieces, mix well, and allow to stand for 30 minutes.

Cover saucepan and place over moderate heat for 10 minutes.

Remove cover, stir, and reduce heat.

In another pan heat oil, fry mustard seed for 2 seconds only, add onion and fry until golden brown.

Add garlic and ginger and fry for 2 minutes, stirring.

Add contents of pan to chicken in saucepan. Add potatoes, and extra water if necessary, and cook until potatoes and chicken are tender.

Reduce heat and add coconut cream mixture. Bring to the boil and boil for further 5 minutes, add lemon juice and stir. Remove from heat and serve.

Serve with rice, vegetables and chutney.

Serves 4–6

BARBECUED CHICKEN PIECES

1 tablespoon worcestershire
  sauce
2 small cloves garlic, crushed
2 teaspoons chilli sauce
  (optional)
$\frac{1}{4}$ teaspoon sesame oil
1 teaspoon sugar
Pinch turmeric
Salt and pepper
4 chicken quarters *or* 8
  chicken pieces
2 teaspoons butter, melted
$\frac{1}{4}$ cup cooking oil
Little lemon juice

In a large bowl, mix worcestershire sauce, garlic, chilli sauce (optional), sesame oil, sugar, turmeric and salt and pepper to taste.

Add chicken and mix well until all pieces are covered with sauce. Cover and allow to stand in the refrigerator for 2 hours.

Place chicken pieces in a baking dish or on a grill and pour over remaining marinade and melted butter. Bake (190°C, 375°F), or grill, until cooked, basting regularly with the oil and pan juices, and turning often.

If desired, lemon juice to taste may be sprinkled over the chicken before serving.

Serve with salad and Coconut Rice (p.71).

Serves 4

Note: Chicken may also be cooked on an outdoor barbecue.

CHICKEN LIVERS IN SAUCE

750 g (1$\frac{1}{2}$ lb) chicken livers
Salt and pepper
$\frac{1}{2}$ teaspoon sesame oil
6 tablespoons cooking oil
1 large onion, cut into 15
  mm ($\frac{1}{2}$ in) slices
Thin slice ginger, shredded
2 tablespoons soy sauce
2 tablespoons worcestershire
  sauce

Place chicken livers in a bowl, sprinkle with salt and pepper and sesame oil, mix well and allow to stand for 10 minutes.

Heat cooking oil in a pan, fry onion gently until soft and lightly browned.

Add ginger and chicken livers to pan and fry until livers are cooked, stirring often to prevent burning.

Add soy sauce and worcestershire sauce to pan, mix well, and remove.

Serve with toast or rice, and chutney.

Serves 4–6

CHICKEN IN LENTILS AND BEANS

1 cup lentils
2½ cups water
1 chicken, cut into serving
  pieces
2 cloves garlic, chopped
5 mm (¼ in) slice fresh
  ginger, chopped
Salt
1½ tablespoons coriander *or*
  curry powder
½ teaspoon chilli powder
  (optional)
¼ teaspoon turmeric
2 medium potatoes,
  quartered and boiled
2 tablespoons cooking oil
½ teaspoon mustard seed
2 large onions, sliced thinly
2 fresh green chillies, halved
  (optional)
½ cup frozen green peas
½ cup frozen or canned lima
  beans
½ cup frozen or canned corn
  kernels
1 ripe tomato, quartered
Few mint leaves (optional)
Garnish: leaves of 2 shallots,
  chopped
  2 sprigs parsley, chopped

Put lentils and 1½ cups water into a large saucepan, bring to the boil and boil gently until lentils are soft. Put aside.

Put chicken pieces and remaining water in large saucepan, add garlic, ginger, salt, coriander, chilli powder (optional) and turmeric. Bring to the boil, reduce heat and simmer until chicken is tender.

Add the boiled lentils and potatoes to the chicken, remove saucepan from heat and put aside.

In a large frying pan heat cooking oil, add mustard seed and fry for 5 seconds only. Add onions and fry gently until golden brown. Add chillies, peas, lima beans, corn and tomato, mix well and fry for 3 minutes.

Add boiled chicken, potatoes and lentils to pan and stir gently, being careful not to break the chicken, potatoes, or beans. Add extra water if necessary. Bring mixture to the boil and add mint leaves (optional).

Pour into deep dish, garnish with chopped shallot leaves and parsley, and serve.

Serves 6–8

DUCK CURRY

2 tablespoons cooking oil
1 large onion, chopped
2 cloves garlic, pounded
Thin slice ginger, pounded
1 tablespoon coriander *or*
  curry powder
1 teaspoon chilli powder
  (optional)
½ teaspoon cummin
¼ teaspoon turmeric
¼ teaspoon fenugreek seed,
  pounded
¼ teaspoon mustard seed,
  pounded
1 duck, cut into large pieces
½ cup water
Salt
½ cup canned coconut milk
  or 60 g (2 oz) coconut
  cream mixed with ½ cup
  water, *or* evaporated milk

Heat oil in a deep saucepan, add onions and fry until lightly browned.

Add garlic, ginger, coriander, chilli powder (optional), cummin, turmeric, fenugreek powder and mustard seed. Fry for 10 seconds only, then add duck pieces and fry for a further 5 minutes. Add water, salt to taste, and finally coconut milk. Cover pan and bring to the boil. Reduce heat and boil gently until duck is tender and gravy is thick. Pour curry into a dish and serve with plain rice or Yellow Rice (p. 72), and salad.

Serves 4–6

SPICY HOT ROAST DUCK

1 duck, cut in half
1 tablespoon coriander *or*
  curry powder
½ teaspoon chilli powder
¼ teaspoon each turmeric,
  cummin, aniseed,
  cinnamon, clove powder,
  cardamom powder
Salt
2 teaspoons vinegar
3 tablespoons cooking oil
2 large onions, cut into 15
  mm (½ in) slices
60 g (2 oz) coconut cream
  mixed with ½ cup water
Garnish: 2 celery leaves,
  chopped

In a large bowl mix coriander, chilli powder, turmeric, cummin, aniseed, cinnamon, clove powder, cardamom powder, salt to taste and vinegar. Add duck halves, rub all over with spice mixture and allow to stand for 15 minutes.

Heat oil in a pan and add onions. Fry until golden brown. Add seasoned duck and mix well.

Transfer contents of pan to a baking dish and pour over coconut cream. Bake in moderate oven until duck is tender and gravy thick.

Remove duck to a warmed platter and garnish with chopped celery leaves.

Serve with plain rice or Yellow Rice (p. 72) and salad.

Serves 4–6

SARA'S HOT SPICY DUCK CURRY

1 duck, cut into serving
    pieces
2 tablespoons coriander *or*
    curry powder
1 tablespoon chilli powder
$\frac{1}{4}$ teaspoon cummin
$\frac{1}{4}$ teaspoon turmeric
$\frac{1}{4}$ teaspoon mustard seed,
    pounded to powder
$\frac{1}{4}$ teaspoon fenugreek seed,
    pounded to powder
Thin slice ginger, pounded
1 clove garlic, crushed
Salt and pepper
3 tablespoons cooking oil
2 large onions, minced
30 g (1 oz) coconut cream
    (optional) mixed with $\frac{1}{2}$
    cup water

In a large bowl, mix coriander, chilli powder, cummin, turmeric, mustard seed, fenugreek seed, ginger, garlic and salt and pepper to taste.

Add duck pieces to spice mixture and mix well to cover on all sides. Allow to stand for 10 minutes. Heat oil in a deep saucepan and fry onions until golden brown. Add seasoned duck pieces to pan, mix well. Cook for 15 minutes over fairly high heat, stirring often, then cover pan and simmer for 15 minutes, stirring occasionally.

Reduce heat to moderate, remove cover, and keep turning and stirring to prevent sticking and burning. Add coconut cream (optional) and water, cover pan and leave to cook until duck is tender and oil rises.

Remove lid and continue to fry duck gently for 5 minutes. Pour into a deep dish and serve.

Serve with rice or bread and salad.

Serves 4–6

DUCK WITH BLACK SAUCE

2 tablespoons coriander *or*
    curry powder
$\frac{1}{2}$ teaspoon white pepper
$\frac{1}{2}$ teaspoon cinnamon
1 teaspoon sugar
1 tablespoon honey
Salt
1 duck, cut into quarters or
    in half
4 tablespoons cooking oil
3 large onions, diced or
    ground
1 clove garlic, crushed
1 tablespoon thick soy sauce
1 tablespoon worcestershire
    sauce
2 tablespoons brandy *or*
    sherry
$\frac{1}{2}$ cup water

In a large bowl, mix coriander, pepper, cinnamon, sugar, honey and salt to taste.

Add duck pieces to bowl and mix well until covered on all sides with curry powder mixture. Allow to stand for 30 minutes.

Heat cooking oil in large frying pan and brown duck pieces on all sides. Remove to a dish and keep warm.

In the remaining oil, fry onions until lightly browned. Add garlic, and fry until lightly browned.

Return duck to pan, reduce heat and add soy sauce, worcestershire sauce, brandy and water. Mix well, cover, and simmer until duck is tender and oil rises. Pour curry into a deep dish and serve hot with bread or Fried Rice (p. 70).

Serves 4–6

DUCK CURRY (MADRAS STYLE)

1 clove garlic, crushed
Thin slice ginger, pounded
2 tablespoons coriander *or* curry powder
$\frac{1}{2}$ teaspoon chilli powder (optional)
Pinch cummin
Salt and pepper
Pinch turmeric powder
15 mm ($\frac{1}{2}$ in) piece cinnamon stick, broken, *or* $\frac{1}{4}$ teaspoon cinnamon powder
1 teaspoon tamarind juice *or* vinegar
1 teaspoon mustard seed, pounded
1 tender duck, cut into serving pieces
3 tablespoons cooking oil
1 large onion, chopped
$\frac{1}{4}$ cup water
Garnish: few leaves coriander *or* Chinese celery, chopped

In a large bowl, mix garlic, ginger, coriander, chilli powder (optional), cummin, salt and pepper to taste, turmeric, cinnamon, tamarind juice and pounded mustard seed.

Add duck pieces to spice mixture and mix well to cover on all sides. Allow to stand for 10 minutes. Heat oil in a frying pan and fry onions until golden brown.

Add seasoned duck pieces to pan, stir well and fry for 15 minutes.

Add water to pan and transfer curry to a deep saucepan. Bring to the boil, then reduce heat and simmer, covered, for 15 minutes.

Remove cover and continue cooking until duck is tender, stirring occasionally. When duck is cooked, stir until oil rises.

Remove curry to a serving dish, and garnish with chopped coriander or Chinese celery leaves.

Serve with rice or bread.

Serves 4–6

MEAT

In India, because beef and pork are forbidden to many people on religious grounds, most meat dishes are based on lamb, mutton or goat meat. Lamb dishes are therefore placed first in this chapter, followed by beef, then pork. Then come a number of recipes in which any meat may be used. The recipes range from the simple to the complicated, from hot and spicy to mild and include grills, roasts, stews and fried dishes. Other meat dishes may be found in the Savouries and Rice chapters.

LAMB WITH LENTILS
Dhall-cha

½ cup red lentils
2 cups water
3 tablespoons cooking oil
2 medium onions, sliced finely
1 clove garlic, chopped finely
Thin slice ginger, pounded
500 g (1 lb) leg of lamb, cut into desired pieces
1 tablespoon coriander *or* curry powder
½ teaspoon cummin
¼ teaspoon aniseed
¼ teaspoon turmeric
2½ cups water
2 potatoes, peeled and quartered
2 aubergines (eggplants), peeled and quartered
'1 teaspoon tamarind paste *or* 6 tablespoons tamarind water
Salt
2 fresh green chillies, halved

Put lentils and water in a saucepan, bring to the boil, reduce heat and boil until lentils are soft. Remove lentils and put aside.

In another saucepan, heat oil, add onions and fry until golden brown.

Add garlic, ginger, lamb, coriander, cummin, aniseed, turmeric and water, mix well and bring to the boil. Boil for 10 minutes, covered.

Remove lid, add potatoes and boil for 5 minutes. Add aubergines and boiled lentils and continue to boil until potatoes and aubergines are cooked but still quite firm.

Mix well and add tamarind paste, salt to taste and green chillies. Bring to boil and remove from heat. Stir well and serve, with plain rice or Yellow Rice (p. 72).

Serves 4

LAMB SAMBAL

3 tablespoons cooking oil
2 onions, pounded
2 teaspoons chilli paste
1 teaspoon shrimp paste
2 teaspoons sugar
500 g (1 lb) leg of lamb, cut
    into thin slices or as
    desired
Salt
½ teaspoon tamarind paste
½ cup water

Heat cooking oil in a frying pan, add pounded onions and fry until lightly brown.
Add chilli paste, shrimp paste, sugar, lamb slices and salt to taste. Fry for 5 minutes, stirring and turning, then add tamarind paste and water.
Simmer until meat is tender and oil rises, then remove to a plate.
Serve hot with rice or bread.

Serves 4

LAMB SAMBAL WITH QUAIL EGGS

750 g (1½ lb) lean lamb, cut
    into 25 mm (1 in) cubes
Salt
2 tablespoons coriander *or*
    curry powder
1 tablespoon chilli powder
    (optional)
¼ teaspoon turmeric
1 cup water
2 tablespoons cooking oil
1 large onion, sliced
2 cloves garlic, shredded
Thin slice ginger, pounded
1 large tomato, cubed
2 tablespoons tomato paste
1 teaspoon sugar
40 mm (1½ in) cinnamon
    stick *or* ¼ teaspoon of
    cinnamon powder
2 cardamom pods, pounded
¼ teaspoon cummin
2 sprigs coriander
2 tablespoons evaporated
    milk
2 fresh green chillies, halved
12 quail eggs *or* 6 small
    chicken eggs, hard-boiled
1 tablespoon lemon juice

In a large saucepan, mix lamb cubes with salt to taste, coriander, chilli powder (optional), turmeric and water. Mix well, cover, and bring to the boil. Reduce heat and boil gently until meat is tender. Remove pan from heat and put aside.
Heat oil in large frying pan, add onion, and fry until golden brown.
Add garlic, ginger, tomato, tomato paste, sugar, cinnamon, pounded cardamom, cummin, coriander, evaporated milk and green chillies, and mix well.
Keep stirring slowly and fry until oil appears on the surface.
Add boiled lamb with any gravy left in saucepan. Mix well.
Add eggs and lemon juice. Stir again slowly until oil rises again. Mix well and serve.
Serve with plain rice, Pilau (p. 74) or bread.

Serves 4–6

Beef Malaysian Style (p. 55). Overleaf: *left*—Coconut Milk Curry (p. 35): *right*—Kabab (p. 61) with Yellow Rice (p. 72) and Cucumber and Tomato Salad (p. 88).

SPICY LAMB CHOPS

12 lamb chops
Salt and pepper
1 tablespoon cornflour
2 cloves garlic, crushed
$\frac{1}{4}$ teaspoon Maggi seasoning
$\frac{1}{4}$ teaspoon ginger wine
4 tablespoons cooking oil
1 large onion, sliced
$\frac{1}{4}$ cup water
$\frac{1}{2}$ teaspoon fruit sauce
1 teaspoon worcestershire
   sauce
1 tablespoon tomato paste
   (optional)
1 tablespoon chilli sauce
   (optional)
$\frac{1}{2}$ teaspoon tomato sauce
1 tablespoon mayonnaise

Wash chops, remove excess fat, and place in a bowl. Add pepper and salt to taste, cornflour, garlic, Maggi seasoning and ginger wine, mix well and allow to stand for 10 minutes.

Heat oil in frying pan, add seasoned lamb chops, fry until cooked and brown and put aside.

Put 1 tablespoon of remaining oil into another pan, add onion and fry until lightly browned.

Add water, fruit sauce, worcestershire sauce, tomato paste (optional), chilli sauce (optional) and tomato sauce, mix well, and simmer for 10 minutes.

Add fried chops and mayonnaise, fry for 2 minutes, remove to a platter and serve.

Serve with toast, rice or potatoes.

Serves 6–12

FRIED CRISPY LAMB

1 kg (2 lb) leg of lamb, cut
   into 25 mm (1 in) cubes
2 tablespoons cornflour
2 tablespoons plain flour
2 eggs, beaten
Salt and pepper
1 tablespoon coriander *or*
   curry powder
$\frac{1}{2}$ teaspoon paprika
$\frac{1}{2}$ teaspoon ginger wine
$\frac{1}{4}$ teaspoon clove powder
$\frac{1}{4}$ teaspoon cinnamon
1 cup cooking oil
Garnish: 1 tomato, sliced
   1 cucumber, peeled and
   sliced

Put lamb cubes in a bowl, add cornflower, plain flour, beaten eggs, salt and pepper to taste, coriander, paprika, ginger wine, clove powder and cinnamon. Mix well and allow to stand for 15 minutes.

In a frying pan, heat oil and deep-fry lamb pieces, a few at a time, until golden brown and crisp. Drain and remove to a warmed platter.

Garnish with tomato slices and cucumber slices, and serve hot with rice.

Serves 4–6

Note: This dish can also be served as a savoury, with chilli sauce as a dip.

Beef with Onions and Potatoes (p. 55).

LAMB IN YOGHURT

2 tablespoons cooking oil
4 large onions, sliced finely
Thin slice ginger, shredded
1 clove garlic, chopped
    finely
750 g (1½ lb) leg of lamb,
    cut into pieces 50 mm
    (2 in) square by 25 mm
    (1 in) thick, or as desired
1 pinch turmeric
2 tablespoons coriander *or*
    curry powder
1 tablespoon chilli powder
    (optional)
¼ teaspoon clove powder
¼ teaspoon cinnamon
½ cup natural yoghurt
2 celery leaves *or* sprigs
    coriander leaves, chopped

Heat oil in a saucepan, add onions and fry until golden brown.

Add ginger, garlic, lamb pieces, turmeric, coriander, chilli powder (if hot curry is required), clove powder and cinnamon. Mix well. Cover and simmer on low heat until meat is half done, stirring occasionally to prevent burning.

Add yoghurt, bring to the boil and simmer until meat is cooked and gravy thickens.

Add chopped celery or coriander leaves and remove from heat.

Serve hot with rice and vegetables.

Serves 4

LAMB IN CHILLI SAUCE

1 tablespoon cooking oil
1 onion, chopped finely
Thin slice ginger, chopped
    finely
500 g (1 lb) leg of lamb, cut
    into thin, narrow slices
3 tablespoons tomato sauce
1 chicken stock cube
Salt and pepper
1 tablespoon chilli sauce
1 tablespoon cornflour
    mixed with 2 tablespoons
    cold water
Garnish: 5 lettuce leaves

Heat oil in a frying pan and fry onion and ginger until lightly browned.

Add lamb slices and fry for 15 minutes, then add tomato sauce, chicken stock cube, salt and pepper to taste, chilli sauce and cornflour paste. Mix well and cook for a further 5 minutes, stirring constantly.

Remove from heat, place lamb on lettuce bed and serve.

Serves 4

ARABIAN MUTTON CURRY

1 kg (2 lb) mutton *or* lamb
  or hogget chops
Thin slice ginger, chopped
2 cloves garlic, chopped
Salt
$\frac{1}{4}$ cup slivered almonds
3 fresh green chillies,
  chopped roughly
2 celery leaves,
  chopped roughly
$\frac{1}{4}$ teaspoon black pepper
1 tablespoon vinegar
$\frac{1}{4}$ teaspoon each turmeric,
  clove powder, cinnamon,
  cardamom powder
$\frac{1}{4}$ teaspoon mustard seed,
  pounded coarsely
2 tablespoons coriander
2 tablespoons cooking oil
1 large onion, chopped
  finely
$\frac{1}{2}$ cup natural yoghurt

Remove fat from mutton chops and place them in a bowl.

In a blender or mortar, mix ginger, garlic, salt to taste, almonds, chillies and celery leaves. Blend or pound into a paste.

Pour paste into the bowl of mutton chops. Mix well then add black pepper, vinegar, turmeric, clove powder, cinnamon, cardamom powder, mustard seed and coriander. Mix well and put aside.

In a frying pan, heat cooking oil, fry onions until golden brown, then add seasoned mutton chops. Fry for 10 minutes, turning constantly to prevent sticking and burning.

Reduce heat to low, fry for 5 minutes, and add yoghurt. Stir and mix well. Continue frying gently until mutton is tender and oil appears.

Serve with rice and salad.

Serves 4–6

Note: This is a dry curry, and there should be no gravy.

SLICED BEEF IN TOMATO SAUCE

1 kg (2 lb) rump *or* topside
  or round steak, sliced
$\frac{1}{2}$ teaspoon black pepper
$\frac{1}{2}$ teaspoon paprika (optional)
Thin slice ginger, pounded
1 tablespoon vinegar
3 tablespoons cooking oil
2 large onions, cut into 15
  mm ($\frac{1}{2}$ in) slices
2 tablespoons tomato paste

Put steak slices in a bowl with black pepper, paprika (optional), ginger and vinegar and allow to stand for 15 minutes.

Heat oil in a large frying pan, add onions, and fry until lightly browned.

Add tomato paste and seasoned beef, mix well, and keep frying and turning until meat is tender and oil appears.

Serve with rice or toast.

Serves 4–6

BEEF BALL CURRY

Beef Balls
1 kg (2 lb) minced steak
1 large onion, chopped
    finely
Thin slice ginger, minced
1 teaspoon coriander *or*
    curry powder
Salt and pepper
$\frac{1}{4}$ teaspoon clove powder
$\frac{1}{4}$ teaspoon cinnamon
$\frac{1}{4}$ teaspoon turmeric
1 slice white bread, soaked
    in water and squeezed out

Gravy
2 tablespoons coriander *or*
    curry powder
$\frac{1}{2}$ teaspoon paprika
3 tablespoons cooking oil
1 large onion, chopped
Thin slice ginger, chopped
125 g (4 oz) coconut cream
    mixed with 2 cups water
    or 1 cup evaporated milk
    mixed with 1 cup water
1 large, ripe tomato, cubed
1 tablespoon tomato paste
Curry leaf (optional)
$\frac{1}{4}$ teaspoon cinnamon
$\frac{1}{4}$ teaspoon clove powder
$\frac{1}{4}$ teaspoon cardamom
    powder
1 tablespoon vinegar

Mix all beef ball ingredients thoroughly in a bowl. Make into small, firm balls and put aside.
In a small bowl mix coriander and paprika, and put aside.
Heat oil in a large saucepan, add onion, and fry until golden brown.
Add ginger, coconut cream, tomato, tomato paste, curry leaf (optional), cinnamon, clove and cardamom powders, vinegar, and the coriander and paprika mixture. Mix well.
Bring to the boil and boil gently for 5 minutes, then add prepared beef balls one by one. Continue to cook on a low heat until meat is cooked and gravy thickens. Add extra water if necessary, to prevent curry drying.
Serve hot with Yellow Rice (p. 72) or bread.

Serves 8

Note: Cubed potatoes and carrots may be added with beef balls, if desired.

BEEF MALAYSIAN STYLE

750 g (1½ lb) topside steak
   cut into 25 mm (1 in)
   cubes
¼ teaspoon white pepper
¼ teaspoon cinnamon
¼ teaspoon clove powder
Salt
1 teaspoon sugar
3 tablespoons cooking oil
1 large onion, cut into 15
   mm (½ in) slices
Thin slice ginger, shredded
1 tablespoon chilli sauce
   (optional)
¼ cup water
2 tablespoons soy sauce
Leaves of 3 shallots, chopped
½ cucumber, peeled and
   cubed (optional)

Put beef in a bowl, add white pepper, cinnamon, clove powder, salt to taste, and sugar and mix well. Heat oil in a large pan, add onion and fry until lightly browned.

Add ginger, seasoned beef, chilli sauce (optional) and water and mix well. Bring to the boil, reduce heat and simmer, covered, until meat is tender. Remove lid, add soy sauce and fry until gravy is thick.

Add shallot leaves and cucumber cubes (optional), mix well and serve.

Serve with rice and salad.

Serves 4–6

BEEF WITH ONIONS AND POTATOES

½ cup cooking oil
4 large onions, sliced into 15
   mm (½ in) thick rings
5 mm (¼ in) slice ginger,
   pounded
4 cloves
25 mm (1 in) cinnamon stick
1 tablespoon ground black
   pepper
2 tablespoons tomato paste
1 kg (2 lb) blade steak, cut
   into 25 mm (1 in) cubes
20 whole, small new
   potatoes, boiled and
   peeled if desired
Salt

Heat cooking oil in a large saucepan, add onions and fry until lightly browned.

Add ginger and fry for 5 seconds only, then add cloves, cinnamon stick, black pepper, tomato paste and steak cubes and fry for 5 minutes, stirring constantly.

Add potatoes and salt to taste, mix well, cover saucepan and simmer for 10 minutes.

Remove lid and continue cooking, stirring occasionally, until meat is cooked and oil comes to top.

Serve hot with rice and vegetables.

Serves 6

SPICY BEEF STEAK

750 g (1½ lb) rump *or*
    topside *or* round steak,
    15 mm (½ in) thick, cut
    into 100 mm (4 in)
    squares
Thin slice ginger, pounded
2 fresh green chillies,
    chopped coarsely
¼ teaspoon clove powder
¼ teaspoon cinnamon
¼ teaspoon turmeric
Salt
Black pepper
1 tablespoon vinegar
¼ cup water
3 tablespoons cooking oil

In a large saucepan, mix steak pieces, ginger, chillies, clove powder, cinnamon, turmeric, salt and black pepper to taste, vinegar and water. Allow to stand for 5 minutes.

Cover and slowly bring to boil. Reduce heat and simmer until water is absorbed and meat is cooked. Remove lid, add cooking oil, and gently fry meat for 10 minutes, turning all the time.

Remove from heat, pour into serving dish and serve with rice or bread.

Serves 4

Note: This is a dry curry and there should be no gravy.

BEEF WITH EGGS

2 tablespoons cooking oil
1 onion minced
Thin slice ginger, minced
250 g (½ lb) lean beef, cut
    into thin strips
Salt and pepper
¼ teaspoon cinnamon
¼ teaspoon clove powder
¼ teaspoon turmeric
½ teaspoon ginger wine
4 eggs, beaten well

Heat oil in a large frying pan, add onion and fry until golden brown.

Add ginger, beef strips, salt and pepper to taste, cinnamon, clove powder, turmeric and ginger wine. Mix well. Fry and turn for 10 minutes, until meat is cooked.

Spread beaten eggs on meat. Let the omelette set for 5 minutes then turn and fry other side until cooked.

Serve hot with rice or on toast.

Serves 4

MINCED PORK BALLS WITH YOGHURT SAUCE

Pork balls
1 kg (2 lb) minced pork
Pinch pepper (or more if
    desired)
1 clove garlic, minced finely
Thin slice ginger, minced
    finely
Pinch turmeric
1 fresh green chilli *or* $\frac{1}{2}$
    capsicum, minced finely
$\frac{1}{2}$ teaspoon garam masala
Salt
1 slice white bread, soaked
    in water and squeezed out
1 cup cooking oil

Sauce
4 tablespoons cooking oil
1 large onion, chopped
    finely
1 clove garlic, pounded
Thin slice ginger, pounded
2 tablespoons coriander *or*
    curry powder
1 tablespoon tomato paste
1 large ripe tomato,
    quartered
$\frac{1}{4}$ teaspoon cinnamon
$\frac{1}{4}$ teaspoon clove powder
$\frac{1}{4}$ teaspoon turmeric
$\frac{1}{2}$ teaspoon paprika (optional)
1 fresh green chilli *or* $\frac{1}{2}$
    capsicum, sliced
1 cup natural yoghurt,
    beaten well

Put minced pork in a bowl, add pepper, garlic, ginger, turmeric, chilli, garam masala, salt to taste and soaked bread and mix well.

Form mixture into balls 25 mm (1 in) in diameter and put aside.

Heat oil in a frying pan, add pork balls and fry until golden brown. Drain well and remove to a plate.

To make sauce, heat cooking oil in a saucepan, add onions and fry until golden brown.

Reduce heat to low and add garlic, ginger, coriander, tomato paste, tomato, cinnamon, clove powder, turmeric, paprika (optional) and chilli.

Stir constantly to prevent burning. Fry, stirring, for 5 minutes.

Add pork balls and yoghurt. Stir gently, cover and simmer for 10 minutes.

Remove from heat and serve with rice or bread and plenty of salad.

Serves 6

PORK CURRY

4 tablespoons cooking oil
½ teaspoon mustard seed
1 large onion, minced
Thin slice ginger, pounded
1 clove garlic, chopped
   finely
4 potatoes, quartered
2 tablespoons coriander *or*
   curry powder
½ teaspoon chilli paste
   (optional)
½ teaspoon pepper
Salt
1 cup water
¼ teaspoon each clove
   powder, cardamom
   powder, cinnamon,
   turmeric, cummin
1 tablespoon tomato paste
750 g (1½ lb) lean pork, cut
   into 25 mm (1 in) cubes
1 teaspoon vinegar

Heat oil in a saucepan, add mustard seed, fry for 2 seconds only, then add onion and fry until golden brown.

Add ginger, garlic, potatoes, coriander, chilli paste (optional), pepper, salt to taste, water, clove powder, cardamom powder, cinnamon, turmeric and cummin. Mix well.

Cover, bring to the boil and boil until potatoes are half cooked, then add tomato paste, pork and vinegar. Mix well.

Reduce heat to low and simmer, covered, until potatoes and pork are cooked.

Remove lid and bring to the boil, then remove pan from heat.

Serve with rice and vegetables.

Serves 4–6

ROAST PORK

1 kg (2 lb) piece pork, with
   fat
1 tablespoon coriander *or*
   curry powder
2 cloves garlic, crushed
¼ teaspoon cinnamon
   powder *or* 15 mm (¼ in)
   piece cinnamon stick
2 tablespoons soy sauce
2 teaspoons sugar
Salt and pepper

(continued)

In a bowl, mix coriander, garlic, cinnamon, soy sauce, sugar, salt and pepper to taste, sesame oil, chicken stock cube, vinegar and monosodium glutamate.

Rub spice mixture all over the pork and allow to stand for 30 minutes.

Place pork in a greased baking tray, sprinkle onion rings over, then cooking oil. Place in hot oven (190°C, 375°F) and bake for 20 minutes. Reduce heat to moderate (175°C, 350°F) and continue to bake until pork is well cooked. Remove pork from

(continued)

½ teaspoon sesame oil
1 chicken stock cube
½ teaspoon vinegar
Pinch monosodium
    glutamate
1 large onion, sliced thickly
    and separated into rings
2 tablespoons cooking oil

oven, carve into bite-sized pieces or as liked, and place on a warmed platter.
Serve with white or brown rice and canned or bottled pickled cucumber.

Serves 4–6

PORK IN TOMATO

1 kg (2 lb) lean pork, cut
    into 25 mm (1 in) cubes
½ teaspoon sugar
Salt and pepper
¼ teaspoon sesame oil
1 clove garlic, pounded
3 tablespoons cooking oil
1 large onion, cubed
1 large tomato, sliced
Thin slice ginger, shredded
2 tablespoons tomato puree
    or tomato paste
1 teaspoon chilli sauce (or
    more if desired)
½ teaspoon vinegar or
    worcestershire sauce
½ cup water
1 tablespoon soy sauce
Leaves of 2 shallots, chopped

Put pork cubes in a bowl, add sugar, salt and pepper to taste and garlic. Mix well and allow to stand for 10 minutes.
Heat oil in a frying pan, add onions and fry until lightly browned.
Add seasoned pork, fry for 2 minutes, then add tomato, ginger, tomato puree, chilli sauce, vinegar and ½ cup water, and stir for 5 minutes.
Cover, bring to the boil, reduce heat and simmer until meat is tender, oil rises and little gravy remains.
Add thick soy sauce and stir for 2 minutes and add chopped shallot leaves.
Remove from heat and serve with rice and bread.

Serves 4

MINCED MEAT CAKE

2 tablespoons oil
1 large onion, minced
Thin slice ginger, minced
1 or 2 fresh green chillies,
    minced (optional)
750 g (1½ lb) minced beef *or*
    lamb
1 teaspoon coriander *or*
    curry powder
¼ teaspoon each cummin,
    cinnamon, cardamom
    powder, turmeric, clove
    powder
½ teaspoon paprika (optional)
Salt and pepper
2 large potatoes, boiled and
    mashed
2 sprigs coriander *or* 2 celery
    leaves, minced finely
2 shallots, chopped finely
½ teaspoon vinegar
1 egg, beaten
Breadcrumbs
1 cup cooking oil (or more
    if needed)
Garnish: 1 small onion,
    sliced finely
    1 tomato, sliced

Heat oil in frying pan, fry onion till lightly brown, then add ginger, chillies (optional) and the minced beef. Mix well.

Add coriander, cummin, cinnamon, cardamom powder, turmeric, clove powder, paprika (optional) and salt and pepper to taste. Stir well and fry for 15 minutes.

Remove pan from heat, pour contents into a bowl and add mashed potatoes, chopped coriander leaves, shallots and vinegar. Mix well.

Form mixture into egg shapes or flat, round cakes. Dip the meat cutlets one by one into the beaten egg, then roll in breadcrumbs and put aside.

Heat cooking oil in a frying pan and fry a few meat cakes at a time until cooked and brown. Drain, pile on a warmed platter and garnish with raw onion and tomato slices.

Serves 4–6

MINCED MEAT CURRY

4 tablespoons cooking oil
2 large onions, chopped
    finely
1 clove garlic, chopped
    finely
Thin slice ginger, shredded
2 potatoes, cut into 15 mm
    (½ in) cubes

Heat oil in a large saucepan, fry onions until golden brown.

Add garlic and ginger and fry for 2 minutes.

Add potatoes, stir, add water and cook gently, covered, for 10 minutes, stirring occasionally.

Add minced meat, cinnamon, clove powder, cardamom powder, turmeric, salt and pepper to taste, coriander, chilli powder, aniseed and cum-

(continued)

(continued)

¼ cup water
750 g (1½ lb) minced beef
  or lamb or pork
¼ teaspoon each cinnamon,
  clove powder, cardamom
  powder, turmeric
Salt and pepper
2 tablespoons coriander or
  curry powder
½ teaspoon chilli powder
½ teaspoon aniseed
½ teaspoon cummin
½ cup frozen peas
125 g (4 oz) coconut cream
  or 4 tablespoons
  evaporated milk

min. Mix well and stir constantly to prevent burning.

Continue frying and stirring until water is absorbed, then add frozen peas and coconut cream or evaporated milk. Mix well.

Cook until peas are cooked and curry is dry, stirring constantly.

Remove to a dish and serve hot with rice and vegetables or bread.

Serves 4–6

Note: 1 tomato, chopped, or 1 teaspoon tomato paste may be added with the peas and coconut cream, if desired.

KABAB

750 g (1½ lb) rump or
  topside steak, leg of lamb
  or chicken, cut into 25
  mm (1 in) cubes
2 tablespoons coriander or
  curry powder
¼ teaspoon pepper
¼ teaspoon turmeric
Thin slice ginger, pounded
¼ teaspoon each cummin,
  clove powder, garam
  masala (optional)
4 tablespoons yoghurt
½ teaspoon chilli powder
  (optional)
1 teaspoon besan flour
½ teaspoon vinegar
2 teaspoons sugar
Salt
1 teaspoon lemon juice
1 tablespoon cooking oil

Place all ingredients in a bowl, mix well, and allow to stand for 15 minutes.

Thread seasoned meat cubes on skewers and put aside for a further 30 minutes.

Grill on coal fire (barbecue) or under a gas or electric griller, basting frequently with extra cooking oil.

When meat is cooked, remove to a platter and serve hot with Kabab Sauce (p. 97) and Cucumber and Pineapple Salad (p. 88).

Serves 4–6

SATAY

1 kg (2 lb) rump *or* topside
or round steak, *or* leg of
lamb *or* chicken *or* lean
pork, cut into bite-size
pieces
2½ tablespoons coriander *or*
curry powder
½ teaspoon aniseed
¼ teaspoon cummin
¼ teaspoon turmeric
1 teaspoon chilli powder
(optional)
2 stalks lemon grass,
pounded
3 thin slices galangal root,
pounded (optional)
1 tablespoon sugar
1 teaspoon tamarind paste *or*
2 tablespoons of thick
tamarind juice
Salt
60 g (2 oz) coconut cream
mixed with ½ cup of
water and 3 tablespoons
cooking oil

Put meat in a bowl and add all remaining
ingredients except coconut cream and oil mixture.
Mix well and allow to stand for 1 hour.
Thread seasoned meat on skewers.
Grill skewered meat on coal fire (barbecue) or gas
or electric grill (a coal fire or barbecue will give the
best flavour). Brush meat with coconut cream and
oil mixture 3 or 4 times during cooking.
Serve with Satay Sauce (p. 96).

Serves 4–6

KURMAH

1 kg (2 lb) topside *or* round
steak *or* lamb *or* chicken,
cut into 50 mm (1 in)
cubes
3 tablespoons coriander *or*
curry powder
¼ teaspoon each cinnamon,
clove powder, cummin,
aniseed, white pepper,
turmeric
2 cardamom pods, crushed
or ¼ teaspoon cardamom
powder

Put meat in a large saucepan with coriander,
cinnamon, clove powder, cummin, aniseed, white
pepper, turmeric, ginger, vinegar, water and salt to
taste. Mix well.
Cover saucepan and cook over a high heat for 10
minutes. Remove lid and continue to cook for a
further 15 minutes.
Add almond paste and stir well to prevent sticking
and burning. Reduce heat to low, add yoghurt and
mix well. Cook until meat is tender and gravy
thickens.
In a large frying pan, heat cooking oil, add onions,
and fry until golden brown.

(continued)

(continued)

Thin slice fresh ginger,
    minced or chopped finely
1 teaspoon vinegar
¼ cup water
Salt
30 whole almonds, peeled
    and ground to a paste
2 cups natural yoghurt
3 tablespoons cooking oil
2 medium onions, sliced
    finely
1 stalk Chinese celery,
    chopped (optional)

Add cooked meat and Chinese celery (optional) to
pan and cook, stirring constantly, for 10 minutes
until gravy is thick and oil rises.
Pour Kurmah into a dish and serve with Vegetable
Rice (p. 72) or Pilau (p. 74) and chutney.

Serves 4–6

MEAT AND COCONUT CURRY

1 kg (2 lb) leg of lamb *or*
    topside *or* round steak
    cut into 25 mm (1 in)
    cubes or as desired
2 tablespoons coriander *or*
    curry powder
½ teaspoon chilli powder
    (optional)
¼ teaspoon black pepper
¼ teaspoon each tur-
    meric, cummin, aniseed,
    cinnamon, clove powder,
    cardamom powder
1 clove garlic, pounded
5 mm (¼ in) slice ginger,
    shredded
1 teaspoon vinegar
2 fresh green chillies, slit
    open (optional)
Salt
3 or 4 curry leaves
½ cup water
2 tablespoons cooking oil
1 large onion, sliced finely
2 ripe tomatoes, quartered
125 g (4 oz) coconut cream
    mixed with 1½ cups water

Put meat in a saucepan, add coriander, chilli
powder (optional), black pepper, turmeric, cummin, aniseed, cinnamon, clove powder, cardamom
powder, garlic, ginger, vinegar, green chillies
(optional), salt to taste, curry leaves and water. Mix
well.
Bring to the boil, reduce heat and boil slowly,
covered, until meat is cooked.
In a frying pan, heat oil, add sliced onion, and fry
until golden brown.
Add tomatoes, toss and turn for 5 seconds, then
pour contents of pan into the boiled meat. Stir
well, add coconut cream and water, and mix again.
Bring to the boil and remove from heat.
Serve hot with rice or bread with salad.

Serves 4–6

Note: Boiled potatoes may be added to the curry
before serving, if desired.

BEEF OR LAMB WITH COCONUT

750 g (1½ lb) topside *or*
  round steak *or* leg of
  lamb, cut into large pieces
  about 15 mm (½ in) thick
  and 50 mm (2 in) square
2 tablespoons coriander *or*
  curry powder
½ teaspoon chilli powder
  (optional)
½ teaspoon black pepper
¼ teaspoon each turmeric,
  cummin, cinnamon,
  cardamom powder, clove
  powder
¼ teaspoon aniseed
Thin slice ginger, shredded
1 teaspoon vinegar
2 curry leaves (optional)
Salt
¼ cup water
2½ tablespoons cooking oil
½ teaspoon mustard seed
  (optional)
2 medium onions, chopped
  or sliced
4 tablespoons desiccated
  coconut

Put meat in a saucepan with coriander, chilli
powder (optional), black pepper, turmeric, cummin, cinnamon, cardamom powder and clove
powder, aniseed, ginger, vinegar, curry leaves, salt
to taste and water. Mix well.
Cover pan, bring to the boil, reduce heat and boil
gently for 15 minutes.
In a frying pan, heat cooking oil, add mustard seed
(optional) and chopped onion and fry until golden
brown.
Add desiccated coconut, fry until light brown.
Pour contents of frying pan into the saucepan, mix
well, and cook gently until dry.
Remove and pour into a dish.
Serve hot with rice and vegetables.

Serves 4

LAMB OR CHICKEN STEW

1 kg (2 lb) lamb, cut into
  25 mm (1 in) cubes *or*
  chicken, minced
1½ tablespoons coriander *or*
  curry powder
¼ teaspoon each cardamom
  powder, aniseed,
  cinnamon, turmeric
Thin slice ginger, sliced
  finely

In a bowl, mix coriander, cardamom powder,
cinnamon, aniseed, turmeric, ginger, salt and black
pepper to taste, vinegar, curry leaves, chillies,
garlic (optional).
Add lamb or chicken to spice mixture, mix well
and allow to stand for 5 minutes.
Transfer contents of pan to a saucepan, fry over a
moderate heat for 10 minutes.
Add potatoes, water and celery, bring to the boil,
reduce heat and boil slowly until the meat and

(continued)

(continued)

Salt
Black pepper
1 teaspoon vinegar
3 or 4 curry leaves
2 fresh green chillies, halved
2 cloves garlic, pounded
   (optional)
2 medium potatoes,
   quartered
4 cups water
1 stalk celery
2 tablespoons cooking oil
$\frac{1}{2}$ teaspoon mustard seed
1 large onion, chopped
125 g (4 oz) coconut cream
   or $\frac{1}{2}$ cup evaporated milk

potatoes are cooked.
In a frying pan heat cooking oil, add mustard seed and fry for 2 seconds, then add onions and fry until golden brown.
Pour contents of frying pan into the saucepan, add coconut cream, mix well and bring to boil. Boil 5 minutes and remove.
Serve hot with bread or plain pancakes.

Serves 4–6

PICKLED MEAT
(Achar)

750 g (1$\frac{1}{2}$ lb) rump *or*
   topside steak *or* leg of
   lamb, cut into 25 mm
   (1 in) cubes
$\frac{1}{2}$ teaspoon pepper
2$\frac{1}{2}$ tablespoons chilli powder
$\frac{1}{4}$ teaspoon turmeric
$\frac{1}{4}$ teaspoon cummin
$\frac{1}{2}$ teaspoon cinnamon
$\frac{1}{2}$ teaspoon clove powder
2 teaspoons sugar
Salt
1 cup cooking oil
1 teaspoon mustard seed,
   coarsely pounded
$\frac{1}{2}$ teaspoon fenugreek seed
   (optional)
Thin slice ginger, chopped
   finely
2 cloves garlic, crushed
$\frac{1}{4}$ cup vinegar

Put meat cubes in a bowl with pepper, chilli powder, turmeric, cummin powder, cinnamon, clove powder, sugar and salt to taste. Mix well and leave to stand for 30 minutes.
Heat oil in frying pan on moderate heat, add mustard seed, fenugreek seed (optional), ginger and garlic and fry for 2 minutes.
Reduce heat and add seasoned meat and vinegar. Mix well. Fry until meat is tender and oil rises to the surface, stirring and turning often to prevent burning.
Remove and cool. Keep in an air-tight bottle in the refrigerator. Will keep for 3 to 4 weeks if necessary.
Serve cold with hot rice or bread.

Serves 4–6

PICKLED MEAT
(*Vindaloo*)

1 kg (2 lb) lean pork, *or* leg
of lamb *or* topside *or*
round steak cut into
desired pieces
1½ teaspoons chilli powder *or*
chilli paste
1 teaspoon cummin
¼ teaspoon turmeric
3 cloves garlic, pounded
Salt and pepper
3 tablespoons vinegar
1 tablespoon sugar
4 tablespoons cooking oil
1 teaspoon mustard seed,
crushed well

In a bowl, mix chilli powder, cummin, turmeric, garlic, salt and pepper to taste, vinegar and sugar. Add pork to spice mixture, mix well and allow to stand for 1 or 2 hours.

Heat oil in a frying pan on a high flame, add crushed mustard then marinated pork, fry for 5 minutes, turning and stirring, and reduce heat to moderate.

Continue to fry and turn until dry and oil rises, then remove and cool.

Serve cold with rice or bread.

Serves 8

Note: This pickled meat will keep for a few days in the refrigerator.

Prawns in Coconut (p. 26) with Zucchini and Potatoes
(p. 79). and Boiled Rice (p. 69).

RICE

Rice is served at every meal in India, and so many different ways of cooking it have been developed. Rice is an ideal accompaniment to curries of all types. It also forms the basis of many dishes, such as pilaus and biryanis. In this chapter I have included some interesting and tasty rice dishes, some which are intended as curry accompaniments, and some which are meals in themselves. I have also included some Chinese-style fried rice recipes, delicious alone or with curry or other meat, and ideal ways of using left-over cooked rice.

RICE VARIETIES

There are many different kinds of rice, all particularly suited to different dishes. They fall into three basic categories: round grain rice, the least known; short grain rice, used in Chinese cooking and for desserts; long grain rice, used as a base for many Indian dishes, and served fried or boiled with curries. The best long grain rice is Basmati, a delicious, aromatic variety which is easily cooked well. It is not stocked everywhere, but health food shops and shops which specialise in Indian foods will certainly be able to supply it.

BROWN RICE

Brown or natural rice is unpolished and must be cooked in more water and for a longer time than polished rice. It has a superb, nutty flavour, and is firmer in texture than white rice. All the recipes in this chapter may be made with brown rice, if the cooking time and the quantity of liquid in which the rice is cooked are increased.

Lamb Biryani (p. 76).

COOKING TIMES

I have not given specific cooking times for these recipes, as every rice cooks at a different speed and has different qualities. It is up to the individual cook to perfect, by trial and error, the method of cooking the rice he or she prefers. Well cooked rice is fluffy and dry, and every grain is separate. It should not be sticky and mushy—sure signs of overcooking and stirring too much. To test whether rice is cooked, rub a grain or two between finger and thumb. If the grains are soft, with no granules, the rice is cooked.

TO REHEAT RICE

Place in a colander over a pan of simmering water, and cover. Stir occasionally with a fork until all rice is hot. *or*
Place in a buttered, ovenproof dish, cover with buttered greaseproof paper (butter side down) and then with lid. Bake in a low to moderate oven (120°C–175°C [250°F–350°F]) for 15 to 20 minutes. *or*
Place in a saucepan, add little water and steam over low heat, covered, for about 5 minutes or until warmed through. Stir with fork or chopstick and remove. *or*
Heat a little oil in a frying pan, add rice, and stir with a fork over low heat until warmed through.

BASIC BOILED RICE (1)

3 cups rice
Water
Salt (optional)

Wash rice thoroughly until water runs clear.
Put rice in saucepan and add cold water to come about 20 mm (¾ in) above the surface of the rice. Add salt to taste, if desired.
Bring to the boil rapidly, then reduce heat to moderate and boil until water has dried up and air bubbles appear on the surface of the rice.
Reduce heat to very low, cover saucepan and simmer for 15 or 20 minutes. Rice is cooked when a few grains rubbed between finger and thumb are soft, with no granules.
Stir gently with a fork, to fluff rice up.
Serve immediately or stand over very low heat until serving time, and stir once again with a fork before serving.

Serves 6–8

BASIC BOILED RICE (2)

3 cups rice, washed and
   drained
3 cups water
Salt (optional)

Put washed rice in saucepan with water and salt to taste (optional). Bring water to the boil as quickly as possible.
Continue to boil until water dries up and air bubbles appear, then immediately reduce heat to very low and cover pan.
Allow rice to simmer for about 20 minutes. Test by rubbing a few grains between finger and thumb. If rice is soft, with no granules, it is cooked.
Pour rice into a colander and stir gently with a fork to fluff it up.
Serve immediately or keep warm until serving time.

Serves 6–8

Note: To cook brown, or natural, rice by this method, increase water to 6 cups, and cook for about 45 minutes. Remember that brown rice never becomes as soft as white. When well cooked it is still rather springy, but not hard.

BASIC BOILED RICE (3)

3 cups rice, washed and
    drained
3½ litres (6 pints) water
2 teaspoons salt (optional)

Put water and salt (optional) into a saucepan and
bring to the boil.
Add rice, slowly so as to keep the water boiling, if
possible.
Boil over high heat, uncovered, for 12–20 minutes,
depending on type of rice, until cooked.
Pour rice into a colander and wash with cold
water.
Place colander over simmering water, covered,
until rice is warm and dry. Stir with a fork, and
serve.

Serves 6–8

BASIC FRIED RICE (1)

½ cup cooking oil
3 cups rice, washed and
    drained
2 teaspoons salt
1½ litres (2½ pints) boiling
    water

In a saucepan, heat oil, add rice and salt and stir
until rice is glazed.
Add boiling water, bring back to the boil, reduce
heat and simmer, uncovered, until almost dry.
Pour contents of pan into an ovenproof dish,
cover, and bake at 120°C (250°F) for about 20
minutes or until cooked.

Serves 4–6

BASIC FRIED RICE (2)

6 cups cold cooked rice
3 tablespoons oil
Salt to taste
Turmeric (optional)
Pepper to taste
1 tablespoon ghee *or* butter
    or margarine

Heat oil in a frying pan, add rice, salt and turmeric
(optional) and stir with a fork until rice is glazed all
over, and heated through.
Sprinkle with pepper, add ghee, and serve.

Serves 4–6

COCONUT RICE

3 cups good long grain rice, washed and drained
140 g (5 oz) coconut cream mixed with 3 cups water *or* 3 cups canned coconut milk
Salt to taste
Garnish: ½ cup raisins, fried until swollen
1 onion, sliced and fried golden brown
6 tablespoons slivered almonds, lightly fried

Put rice, coconut cream and water and salt in a saucepan. Bring to the boil on medium heat, and boil until liquid dries up.

Reduce heat, cover, and continue cooking until rice is well cooked and fluffy. Gently stir with a fork.

Garnish with fried raisins, onion and almonds.

Serve with curry and Cucumber and Pineapple Salad (p. 88).

Serves 4–6

PERSIAN RICE

4½ tablespoons cooking oil
1 large onion, sliced finely
1 clove garlic, sliced finely
Thin slice ginger, chopped finely
4 cups good long grain rice, washed and drained
6 cups water
Salt
Sprig coriander leaves
¼ teaspoon clove powder
¼ teaspoon cinnamon
¼ teaspoon cardamom powder
½ cup evaporated milk
4 tablespoons slivered, blanched almonds, pounded into a paste
125 g (4 oz) coconut cream
Garnish: 1 large onion, sliced and fried golden brown.
¼ cup shredded blanched almonds, lightly fried
½ cup raisins, lightly fried

Heat oil in a large saucepan, add onion and fry until golden brown.

Add ginger and garlic and fry for 2 minutes.

Add rice. Mix well, then add water, salt, bay leaf, clove powder, cinnamon and cardamom powder. Stir and cover, bring to the boil, reduce heat and add evaporated milk, almond paste, and coconut cream. Mix with a fork. Replace lid and cook on a low flame until rice is cooked. Stir with a fork occasionally to prevent burning.

Pour rice into a serving dish and garnish with fried onion, almonds and raisins.

Serve with any curry or chutney with sliced cucumber.

Serves 6

YELLOW RICE

4 cups good long grain rice,
  washed and drained
125 g (4 oz) coconut cream,
  mixed with 6 cups water
Pinch cinnamon
$\frac{1}{4}$ teaspoon turmeric
Salt
2 tablespoons cooking oil
1 large onion, sliced
1 clove garlic, chopped
Thin slice fresh ginger,
  chopped, or $\frac{1}{4}$ teaspoon
  ginger powder
4 tablespoons raisins
Garnish: 1-egg omelette,
  shredded

Put rice in a large saucepan, add coconut cream, cinnamon, turmeric, salt to taste.

In a frying pan, heat oil and fry the onion until golden brown. Remove and put aside.

In the same oil, fry garlic and ginger gently for 2 minutes only, then pour with the remaining oil into the rice.

Bring rice to the boil, reduce heat, and cook, covered, over a moderate flame until rice is three-quarters cooked and half the liquid has been absorbed.

Reduce heat to low and simmer until rice is cooked and liquid has been absorbed. Stir occasionally with a fork to prevent rice from burning.

Lightly fry raisins in a little ghee or oil, add to rice, then add fried onion. Stir rice gently with a fork. Serve on an open platter, garnished with shredded omelette.

Serve with curry, salad and chutney.

Serves 6

VEGETABLE RICE

4 tablespoons cooking oil
1 large onion, chopped
1 clove garlic, chopped
Thin slice ginger, chopped
  finely
1 small carrot, scraped and
  shredded
$\frac{1}{2}$ cup frozen green peas
$\frac{1}{2}$ cup sliced beans
3 cups good long grain rice
$4\frac{1}{2}$ cups water
$\frac{1}{4}$ teaspoon each cinnamon,
  clove powder, cardamom
  powder, cummin,
  turmeric, pepper
1 bay leaf
Salt

In a frying pan, heat oil and fry onion until golden brown.

Add garlic, ginger, carrot, green peas and beans, fry for 10 minutes, stirring, and put aside.

Put the rice in a large saucepan, add water, cinnamon, clove powder, cardamom powder, turmeric, cummin, pepper, bay leaf and salt to taste. Bring to the boil, reduce heat and boil slowly, covered, until water is half absorbed (say 20 minutes).

Add fried ingredients, stir with a fork, and continue cooking until water is absorbed and rice is cooked. Reduce heat to low and stir with a fork, mixing the rice and the fried ingredients well.

Serve with Cucumber and Pineapple Salad (p. 88).

Serves 4–6

TOMATO RICE

4 tablespoons cooking oil
2 large onions, chopped finely
Thin slice ginger, sliced finely
1 clove garlic, sliced finely
2 chicken stock cubes
$\frac{1}{4}$ teaspoon each turmeric, cinnamon, clove powder, cardamom powder, cummin
2 large ripe tomatoes, chopped
4 tablespoons tomato paste
Salt and pepper
3 cups good long grain rice, washed and drained
$4\frac{1}{2}$ cups water
1 bay leaf
$\frac{1}{2}$ cup frozen green peas

Heat oil in a large saucepan, add onions and fry until golden brown.

Add ginger, garlic, chicken stock cubes, turmeric, cinnamon, clove powder, cardamom powder, cummin, tomatoes, tomato paste and salt and pepper to taste, and fry for 10 minutes, stirring often.

Add rice, water and bay leaf, cover saucepan, bring to the boil, reduce heat and boil slowly until water has been absorbed.

Reduce heat to low. Stir rice with fork and add green peas. Cook on a low heat until peas are tender, stirring with a fork occasionally to prevent sticking and burning.

Serve with curry and salad.

Serves 4–6

Note: This dish goes particularly well with Cucumber and Pineapple Salad (p. 88).

RICE WITH RED LENTILS

$3\frac{1}{2}$ tablespoons cooking oil
1 large onion, sliced finely
Thin slice ginger, sliced finely
1 clove garlic, sliced finely
$\frac{1}{4}$ teaspoon cinnamon
$\frac{1}{4}$ teaspoon turmeric
$\frac{1}{4}$ teaspoon clove powder
$4\frac{1}{2}$ cups water (or more if needed)
3 cups good long grain rice, washed and drained
$\frac{1}{2}$ cup red lentils, washed and drained
1 bay leaf
Salt
Garnish: 1 large onion, sliced and fried golden brown

In a large saucepan, heat oil, add onion and fry until golden brown.

Add ginger and garlic and fry for 2 minutes only, then add cinnamon, turmeric, clove powder and water. Mix well.

Add rice, lentils, bay leaf and salt to taste. Cover and simmer on a medium heat.

When water is half absorbed, reduce heat and cook until rice is well done. More water can be added if necessary. Stir occasionally with fork to prevent rice from burning.

Garnish with fried onion.

Serve with curry and Yoghurt with Cucumber (p. 89).

Serves 4–6

CHICKEN PILAU

6 cups water
2 chicken stock cubes
Salt
$\frac{1}{4}$ teaspoon clove powder
$\frac{1}{4}$ teaspoon cinnamon
$\frac{1}{4}$ teaspoon cardamom
   powder
2 bay leaves
4 tablespoons cooking oil
2 large onions, sliced
1 clove garlic, sliced finely
Thin slice ginger, sliced
   finely
1 chicken, cut into serving
   pieces
3 cups good long grain rice,
   washed and drained
4 tablespoons slivered
   blanched almonds, finely
   ground to a paste
2 tablespoons raisins
Garnish: 1 large onion, sliced
   and fried golden brown

In a bowl, mix water, chicken stock cubes, salt to taste, clove powder, cinnamon, cardamom powder and bay leaves and put aside.

In a large saucepan, heat oil, add onions and fry until golden brown.

Add garlic and ginger then the chicken pieces and the water and mixed spices from the bowl. Mix well.

Bring to the boil, reduce heat and boil slowly, covered, for 15 minutes.

Add rice. Cover saucepan, bring back to the boil, reduce heat to moderate, and simmer for 20 minutes.

Reduce heat, add almond paste and stir with a fork. Continue cooking, covered, until rice is cooked and liquid absorbed (rice must be well cooked, so add more water if necessary). Add raisins and stir well with a fork.

Reduce heat and keep warm over a very low flame until ready to serve.

To serve, spread rice and chicken on a platter and garnish with fried onions.

Serve with meat curry or chutney.

Serves 4–6

EGG PILAU

4 tablespoons cooking oil
1 large onion, sliced
$\frac{1}{4}$ cup mixed shredded
   almonds
$\frac{1}{4}$ cup cashew nuts
$\frac{1}{2}$ cup raisins *or* sultanas
1 clove garlic, chopped
   finely
Thin slice ginger, chopped
   finely

In a frying pan, heat 2 tablespoons of the oil, fry onion until golden brown, remove and put aside.

In the same oil, fry almonds and cashews until lightly browned, remove and put aside.

In the same oil, fry raisins until swollen, quickly remove and put aside.

In a large saucepan, melt remaining 2 tablespoons oil and fry garlic and ginger for 2 minutes only.

Add rice, salt and pepper to taste, cinnamon, clove powder, cardamom powder, turmeric, bay leaf

(continued)

(continued)

74   RICE

4 cups good long grain rice, washed and drained
Salt and pepper
$\frac{1}{4}$ teaspoon cinnamon
$\frac{1}{2}$ teaspoon clove powder
$\frac{1}{2}$ teaspoon cardomom powder *or* 3 pods cardamom, crushed
$\frac{1}{4}$ teaspoon turmeric
1 bay leaf
6 cups water
6 eggs, hard-boiled and shelled
Garnish: 1-egg omelette, shredded finely

and water. Mix well.

Bring to the boil, reduce heat to medium and boil, covered, until rice is three-quarters cooked and half the liquid has been absorbed.

Reduce heat to low, add fried onion and hard-boiled eggs. Stir gently with a fork, and continue to cook, covered, until remaining liquid is absorbed and rice is cooked. Stir with a fork occasionally to prevent sticking. Rice must be well cooked, so add a little more water if necessary.

Transfer to serving dish and garnish with fried almonds, cashew nuts and raisins, and shredded omelette.

Serves 6

LAMB PILAU, BEEF PILAU

Make as for Chicken Pilau (p. 74), substituting 1 kg (2 lb) leg of lamb *or* topside *or* round steak for chicken pieces, and beef stock cubes for chicken stock cubes.

FRIED RICE WITH PRAWNS AND EGG

3 tablespoons cooking oil
2 cloves garlic, chopped finely
1 small onion, chopped
Salt and pepper
1 cup cooked prawns
Pinch monosodium glutamate
$\frac{1}{2}$ teaspoon sesame oil
4 cups cooked rice
1-egg omelette, cut into strips
Garnish: 3 shallots, chopped

Heat 3 tablespoons oil, add garlic and fry for 2 minutes, then add onion and fry until golden brown.

Add salt and pepper to taste, then prawns, monosodium glutamate and sesame oil. Mix well.

Add cooked rice, mix well and continue stirring for 5 minutes. Add omelette and stir gently until heated through.

Garnish with chopped shallots and serve hot.

Serves 4

FRIED RICE WITH HAM AND EGGS

2 tablespoons cooking oil
2 cloves garlic, chopped
  finely
1 small onion, chopped
2 eggs, beaten
Salt and pepper
½ teaspoon sesame oil
1 teaspoon soy sauce
125 g (4 oz) ham, cut into
  strips
4 cups cooked rice
125 g (4 oz) cashew nuts,
  fried

Heat oil in a pan, add garlic, then onion, and fry
until golden brown.
Add beaten eggs, salt and pepper to taste, sesame
oil, soy sauce and ham. Fry for 3 minutes, stirring.
Add cooked rice and continue stirring until well
mixed.
Add fried cashew nuts, stir and serve.

Serves 4

FRIED RICE WITH ROAST MEAT AND PEAS

3 tablespoons cooking oil
1 small onion, chopped
500 g (1 lb) roast beef, *or*
  lamb *or* pork cut into
  strips
½ cup frozen green peas
Salt and pepper
1 tablespoon brandy
2 beef stock cubes
1 teaspoon soy sauce
6 cups cooked rice
2-egg omelette, cut into
  strips

Heat oil in a frying pan, add onion and fry until
golden brown.
Add roast beef, peas, salt and pepper to taste,
brandy, beef stock cubes and soy sauce. Mix well.
Add cooked rice. Continue cooking, stirring to
prevent burning, until peas are almost cooked and
beef and rice are hot.
Add omelette, continue cooking and stirring for
further 5 minutes and remove.
Serve with chutney.

Serves 4–6

LAMB BIRYANI

Lamb
1 kg (2 lb) lamb chops
1½ tablespoons coriander *or*
  curry powder
1 teaspoon paprika
¼ teaspoon cummin

Wash lamb, drain well, remove excess fat, place in
a bowl.
In another bowl mix coriander, paprika, cummin,
aniseed, turmeric, cinnamon, cardamom powder,
clove powder, ginger, garlic, vinegar, lemon juice,
pepper and salt to taste.

(continued)

(continued)

¼ teaspoon aniseed
¼ teaspoon each turmeric,
  cinnamon, cardamom
  powder, clove powder
15 mm (½ in) slice ginger,
  pounded
2 cloves garlic, crushed
1 tablespoon vinegar
1 teaspoon lemon juice
¼ teaspoon white pepper
Salt
3 tablespoons cooking oil
4 large onions, chopped
  finely
10 almonds, pounded into a
  paste
6 tablespoons natural
  yoghurt

Rice
4 cups good long grain rice,
  washed and drained
3 tablespoons ghee *or* butter
  or cooking oil
2 onions, sliced finely
Thin slice ginger, shredded
1 clove garlic, shredded
6 cups water
¼ teaspoon each
  turmeric, cinnamon,
  cardamom powder, clove
  powder
1 bay leaf
Salt
4 tablespoons evaporated
  milk
Garnish: 1 large onion, sliced
  and fried golden brown
  125 g (4 oz) cashew nuts,
  fried lightly

Add spice mixture to lamb and mix well. Allow to stand for 15 minutes.
Heat 3 tablespoons cooking oil in a pan. Fry onions till golden brown and pour into a saucepan, then add marinated meat.
Cover saucepan and simmer with no added water for 40 minutes.
Remove from heat, add almond paste and yoghurt. Stir to prevent sticking. Cook, covered, until liquid has dried up and oil rises.
Remove saucepan from heat and put aside.
In a large saucepan, melt 3 tablespoons ghee and fry onions until golden brown.
Add ginger and garlic and fry for 2 minutes.
Add rice, water, turmeric, cinnamon, cardamom powder, clove powder, bay leaf and salt to taste. Mix well. Bring to the boil.
Boil, covered, until rice is three-quarters cooked, then reduce heat to low, add evaporated milk, and continue to cook until remaining liquid is absorbed.
Remove cover, stir rice with a fork, then remove from heat.
Transfer half the rice to a serving dish or casserole. Spread half the curried lamb over it. Make another layer of rice, and top dish with remaining lamb. Cover and keep warm until serving time.
Garnish with fried onion rings and cashew nuts. Serve with chutney and Cucumber and Pineapple Salad (p. 88).

Serves 6

Note: This dish may be made ahead of time and stored in the refrigerator in its casserole dish. To reheat, sprinkle a little water over and place, uncovered, in a medium oven (180°C, 350°F) until warmed through.

VEGETABLES

Many people in India are vegetarian and therefore great attention has been paid to the cooking of vegetables as Indian cookery has developed. I have included just a few recipes here, varying from the very simple, ideal as accompaniments to meat, fish or chicken dishes, to the more complicated and filling dishes which with bread or rice, and perhaps salad and chutney, can be meals in themselves. I have included only those vegetables which are readily available in Western countries, and certainly you may like to experiment with other vegetables and combinations. In the mixed vegetable dishes, particularly, you should feel free to add any vegetables you have on hand, or leave out any you do not.

I have included in this chapter two recipes for the cooking of lentils. Lentils are inexpensive, filling and high in protein, and form the basis of many Indian dishes. The recipes I have given are very simple, and these dishes may be served alone with rice or bread, or as an accompaniment to a meat curry.

SPICED AUBERGINE

3 tablespoons cooking oil
1 large onion, chopped
2 cloves garlic, pounded
2 large potatoes, cut into 15 mm ($\frac{1}{2}$ in) cubes
$\frac{1}{2}$ cup water
$\frac{1}{4}$ teaspoon pepper
$\frac{1}{4}$ teaspoon cummin
$\frac{1}{4}$ teaspoon turmeric
$\frac{1}{4}$ teaspoon garam masala
$\frac{1}{2}$ teaspoon chilli powder (optional)
Salt
2 large aubergines (egg-plants), cut into 15 mm ($\frac{1}{2}$ in) cubes and soaked in cold water
2 tablespoons tomato paste
$\frac{1}{2}$ teaspoon vinegar

Heat oil in a large saucepan, add onion and fry until golden brown.
Add garlic, potatoes, water, pepper, cummin, turmeric, garam masala, chilli powder (optional) and salt to taste. Mix well, cover, bring to the boil and boil for 10 minutes.
Add aubergine, tomato paste and vinegar, and continue cooking until aubergine and potatoes are tender. Stir often to prevent burning.
When liquid has been absorbed and oil rises, remove from heat and serve with rice and chutney.

Serves 6

SPICED CAULIFLOWER

2½ tablespoons cooking oil
1 onion, chopped
2 cloves garlic, pounded
2 potatoes, cut into 25 mm
  (1 in) cubes
¼ teaspoon turmeric
¼ teaspoon cummin
¼ teaspoon clove powder
¼ teaspoon cinnamon
Salt and pepper
½ cup water
500 g (1 lb) cauliflower, cut
  into large chunks
1 carrot, scraped and sliced
  thickly
½ cup green peas

Heat oil in saucepan, fry onions until golden brown, add garlic and fry until light brown.
Add potatoes, turmeric, cummin, clove powder, cinnamon and salt and pepper to taste. Mix well.
Add water, bring to the boil, reduce heat and simmer until potatoes are half cooked.
Add cauliflower, carrot rings and peas, stir gently. Replace lid and simmer until vegetables are cooked, water is absorbed and oil rises. Stir and remove from heat.
Serve with rice or bread.

Serves 4

ZUCCHINI AND POTATOES

4 tablespoons cooking oil
1 onion, chopped finely
1 clove garlic, chopped
4 potatoes, peeled, boiled
  and cut into 25 mm (1 in)
  cubes
1 teaspoon paprika
Salt and pepper
¼ teaspoon each turmeric,
  cummin, cinnamon, clove
  powder and cardamom
  powder
500 g (1 lb) zucchini
  (courgettes), sliced thinly
  lengthways, then into
  pieces 25 mm (1 in) long
1 tomato, diced
1 teaspoon vinegar *or* lemon
  juice (optional)
Leaves of 2 shallots, chopped

Heat oil in a deep frying pan, add onions and fry until golden brown.
Add garlic, then potatoes, paprika, salt and pepper to taste, turmeric, cummin, cinnamon, and clove and cardamom powders and fry for 15 minutes stirring frequently.
Add zucchini and continue to fry, stirring, for 10 minutes.
Add tomatoes, vinegar (optional) and chopped shallot leaves. Continue frying for 5 minutes, stirring frequently to prevent burning, then remove to a serving dish.
Serve hot with rice or bread.

Serves 6

CABBAGE IN COCONUT

2 tablespoons cooking oil
½ teaspoon mustard seed
1 large onion, chopped
1 clove garlic, crushed
   (optional)
¼ teaspoon cummin
¼ teaspoon turmeric
10 cabbage leaves, washed,
   drained and shredded
   finely
2 fresh green chillies,
   chopped coarsely
2 curry leaves
2 tablespoons desiccated
   coconut
Salt

Heat oil in a frying pan on moderate heat, add mustard seed and fry for 2 seconds only, then add onions and fry until golden brown.
Add garlic (optional), cummin, turmeric, shredded cabbage, chillies, curry leaves and desiccated coconut and salt to taste and mix well. Cover and continue cooking for 5 minutes.
Remove lid and continue frying, stirring constantly, until cabbage is cooked and water has been absorbed.
Serve hot with rice and curry.

Serves 4

MIXED VEGETABLE CURRY

60 g (2 oz) cooking oil
1 large onion, chopped
1 clove garlic, pounded
1 tablespoon coriander *or*
   curry powder
4 potatoes, peeled and cut
   into 25 mm (1 in) cubes
½ cup water
2 tomatoes, chopped finely
2 teaspoons tomato paste
1 carrot, scraped and sliced
250 g (½ lb) cabbage,
   shredded
125 g (¼ lb) green beans,
   sliced
Salt
1 celery leaf, chopped

In a large saucepan, heat oil, add onions and fry until golden brown.
Add garlic and fry until lightly browned.
Reduce heat, add coriander, potatoes and water, mix well, cover saucepan and boil for 10 minutes.
Remove lid, add tomatoes, tomato paste, carrot, cabbage, beans and salt to taste and allow to simmer for 10 minutes or until cooked. If gravy is required, add more water.
Add chopped celery leaf, stir and remove from heat.
Serve with rice or bread.

Serves 4

HOT SPICY VEGETABLES

2 tablespoons cooking oil
1 onion, chopped
1 clove garlic, pounded
2 large potatoes, cut into
  quarters
½ cup water
¼ teaspoon turmeric
¼ teaspoon cummin
1 teaspoon paprika
2 tablespoons coriander *or*
  curry powder
2 tablespoons tomato paste
1 small tin lima beans,
  drained
1 turnip, scraped and diced
2 carrots scraped and sliced
  or 6 whole baby carrots,
  scraped if necessary
250 g (½ lb) green beans,
  sliced if desired
250 g (½ lb) green peas
Salt
1 tablespoon canned coconut
  milk *or* 15 g (½ oz)
  coconut cream mixed
  with 1 tablespoon water
  or 1 tablespoon evaporated
  milk
1 tablespoon lemon juice

Heat oil in a large saucepan, add onion and fry until golden brown.

Add garlic and fry until lightly browned.

Add potatoes, water, turmeric, cummin, paprika, coriander and tomato paste and cook, stirring occasionally, for 5 minutes.

Cover and simmer for 10 minutes, removing lid to stir occasionally, to prevent burning.

Add lima beans, turnip, carrots, beans, peas and salt to taste, replace lid and continue cooking until water is absorbed.

Add evaporated milk and lemon juice, stir and fry until curry is dry.

Remove to a dish and serve hot with rice or bread.

Serves 4–6

EGG CURRY WITH POTATOES

3 tablespoons cooking oil
$\frac{1}{4}$ teaspoon mustard seed
2 large onions, chopped
2 cloves garlic, chopped
Thin slice ginger, chopped
    or pounded
1 large ripe tomato, chopped
$\frac{1}{2}$ teaspoon chilli powder
$3\frac{1}{2}$ tablespoons coriander *or*
    curry powder
$\frac{1}{4}$ teaspoon white pepper
$\frac{1}{4}$ teaspoon each cummin,
    aniseed, turmeric,
    cinnamon, clove powder,
    cardamom powder
2 fresh green chillies, halved
2 curry leaves (optional)
1 tablespoon tomato paste
Salt
4 tablespoons water
4 large potatoes, peeled and
    halved
8 hard-boiled eggs, shelled
125 g (4 oz) coconut cream
    mixed with 1 cup water
1 teaspoon vinegar *or* lemon
    juice

Heat oil in a pan, add mustard seed, fry for 10 seconds only then add onions and fry until golden brown.

Add garlic, ginger and tomato and continue to fry for 10 minutes, stirring occasionally. Pour into a saucepan.

In a bowl, mix chilli powder, coriander, pepper, cummin, aniseed, turmeric, cinnamon, clove powder, cardamom powder, chillies, curry leaves (optional), tomato paste, salt to taste and water to make a paste.

Add paste to the saucepan, mix well. Fry for 5 minutes, add potatoes and cook on moderate heat until potatoes are tender.

Add hard-boiled eggs and coconut cream, stir well, then add vinegar and bring to the boil. Remove from heat and serve.

Serve with rice and vegetables.

Serves 8

TOMATO, EGG AND COCONUT

2 tablespoons cooking oil
$\frac{1}{4}$ teaspoon mustard seed
1 onion, minced
Thin slice ginger, minced
$\frac{1}{4}$ teaspoon turmeric
4 green tomatoes, minced
$\frac{1}{4}$ teaspoon pepper
Salt
2 eggs, beaten
4 tablespoons desiccated
    coconut
3 shallots, minced

Heat oil in frying pan on moderate heat, add mustard seed, fry for 5 seconds only, then add onion, ginger and turmeric and fry for 2 minutes. Add tomatoes, pepper and salt to taste, stir well, then add beaten eggs. Cook, stirring, for 5 minutes.

Add desiccated coconut and spring onions. Continue to fry for 5 minutes, then remove from heat. Serve with rice.

Serves 4

Mixed Salad with Peanut Sauce (p. 87).

SPICED MIXED VEGETABLES

1 cup water
2 carrots, scraped and sliced
½ cup frozen peas
1 cup frozen green beans, sliced
½ cup frozen corn kernels
4 tablespoons cooking oil
1 large onion, chopped
2 cloves garlic, pounded
1 teaspoon paprika
¼ teaspoon turmeric
¼ teaspoon cummin
Salt
¼ teaspoon pepper or to taste
Garnish: 2 shallots, chopped

Put water in a saucepan, bring to the boil and add carrots, peas, green beans and corn. Cover and boil for 6 minutes. Drain and put aside.
Heat oil in frying pan, fry onion until lightly browned, add garlic, then boiled vegetables, paprika, turmeric, cummin, salt to taste and pepper. Stir gently over moderate heat for 5 minutes until oil rises, then remove.
Sprinkle with chopped shallots and serve hot with rice.

Serves 4–6

VEGETABLE SOTHI

4 cups canned coconut milk *or* 315 g (10 oz) coconut cream mixed with 4 cups water
4 cabbage leaves, chopped
1 cup sliced frozen green beans
1 cup bean sprouts
2 fresh green chillies, chopped coarsely
1 tablespoon cooking oil
1 onion, chopped finely
2 curry leaves
¼ teaspoon turmeric
2 tablespoons lime juice
Salt

In a saucepan, mix coconut milk, cabbage, beans, bean sprouts and chillies and put aside.
In a frying pan, heat cooking oil, add chopped onions and fry until golden brown.
Add curry leaves and turmeric and mix well.
Pour contents of pan into coconut milk mixture.
Cover saucepan, bring to the boil and boil until vegetables are tender.
Add lime juice and salt to taste, stir, and remove from heat.
Serve with plain rice.

Serves 6

In jars: Lemon Pickle (p. 95), Mango Pickle (p. 94). In bowls: Mint Chutney (p. 91), Red Tomato Chutney (p. 92), Apple and Pineapple Chutney (p. 92).

RED LENTILS
Dhall

1 cup red lentils
2 cups water
1 clove garlic, chopped or
    crushed
Thin slice ginger, chopped
    or shredded
6 fresh green chillies,
    chopped or minced
Salt
2 tablespoons lemon juice

Wash and drain lentils, put in a saucepan, with water, bring to the boil, reduce heat, and boil slowly until soft. Remove from heat and drain, if necessary.

Put boiled lentils into a blender with garlic, ginger, green chillies and salt to taste. Blend to a thick paste.

Alternatively, add crushed garlic, ginger, chillies and salt to the lentils and mix and mash with wooden spoon until mixture is smooth.

Add lemon juice and mix well.

Pour into a bowl and keep in the refrigerator until required.

Serve with rice and curry.

Serves 4–6

YELLOW LENTILS

1 cup yellow lentils
2 cups water
2 tablespoons cooking oil
$\frac{1}{4}$ teaspoon mustard seed
1 large onion, chopped
1 clove garlic, chopped
2 fresh green chillies, halved
1 tomato, quartered
$\frac{1}{4}$ teaspoon turmeric
$\frac{1}{4}$ teaspoon paprika
Salt
2–3 curry leaves (optional)
60 g (2 oz) coconut cream
    mixed with $\frac{1}{2}$ cup water *or*
    $\frac{1}{2}$ cup canned coconut
    milk
1 tablespoon lemon juice

Put yellow lentils in a large saucepan, with water. Bring to the boil and boil uncovered until lentils are soft. Remove pan from heat and put aside.

Heat oil in a frying pan, add mustard seed and chopped onion and fry until golden brown.

Add garlic, green chillies, tomato, turmeric, paprika, salt to taste and curry leaves (optional). Fry, stirring constantly, for 5 minutes, then pour into boiled lentils. Mix well.

Add liquid cream of coconut. Bring mixture to the boil and add lemon juice.

Serve hot with rice.

Serves 4–6

POTATO CURRY

4 tablespoons cooking oil
$\frac{1}{2}$ teaspoon mustard seed
Few curry leaves (optional)
1 onion, chopped
6 potatoes, peeled, boiled
   and cut into 25 mm (1 in)
   cubes
$\frac{1}{4}$ teaspoon turmeric
$\frac{1}{4}$ teaspoon chilli powder
$\frac{1}{4}$ teaspoon cummin
2 green fresh chillies, halved
$\frac{1}{2}$ teaspoon tamarind paste
1 tablespoon lemon juice
Salt

Heat oil in a large saucepan, add mustard seed, curry leaves (optional) and chopped onion and fry until onion is golden brown.

Add boiled potatoes, turmeric, chilli powder, cummin, green chillies and tamarind paste. Mix well and fry for 5 minutes.

Add lemon juice and salt to taste, mix again and serve.

Serve hot with Puris (p. 24).

Serves 4

SALADS

Cool and tangy salads are the ideal curry accompaniments, providing refreshment and contrast in flavour and texture. The recipes given here are just a few of the thousands of possibilities, but I hope they will give you ideas for others. Almost any vegetables can be used to make an interesting salad, and fresh and canned fruits, such as pineapple, mango and melon also make delicious side dishes. See the Chutneys, Pickles and Sauces chapter for other ideas—many Indian chutneys are not cooked, but are delicious, cool combinations of fresh vegetables and fruits.

Fruit salads are given in the Sweets and Desserts chapter.

VEGETABLE SALAD

Salad
6 lettuce leaves, shredded
1 cucumber, peeled and diced
2 tomatoes, cut into wedges
2 boiled potatoes, cut into 25 mm (1 in) cubes
2 hard-boiled eggs, sliced thickly
1 carrot, scraped, cut into thin rings and boiled *or* left raw and shredded

Sauce
2 tablespoons crunchy peanut butter
½ teaspoon brown sugar
1 tablespoon lime juice
4 tablespoons chilli sauce
1 teaspoon soy sauce
Salt

Mix salad ingredients gently in a salad bowl, preferably a glass bowl as this looks decorative on the table, or arrange on an open platter. Keep in the refrigerator, covered, until required.

Mix sauce ingredients in a bowl to make a thick sauce, and put aside.
To serve, pour sauce over Vegetable Salad or serve separately and dip vegetables in the sauce.
Serve with rice as a side dish.

Serves 4–6

MIXED SALAD WITH PEANUT SAUCE

Salad
2 green apples, peeled
   (optional), and cut into 15
   mm (½ in) cubes
250 g (½ lb) bean sprouts,
   parboiled
2 cups canned or fresh
   pineapple cubes (if canned,
   drain well)
1 cucumber, peeled, seeded
   and diced
4 fried bean curd cakes,
   sliced
½ cup sliced, boiled string
   beans *or* French beans
2 eggs, hard-boiled and
   quartered

Sauce
¼ cup roasted peanuts,
   ground *or* 2 tablespoons
   crunchy peanut butter
2 teaspoons tamarind paste
   mixed with ½ cup water *or*
   2 tablespoons lime juice
½ tablespoon chilli paste *or* 1
   tablespoon chilli sauce
   (optional)
Salt

Mix salad ingredients and put in a bowl or spread on a platter. Keep in a cool place or in the refrigerator until required.

Mix sauce ingredients in a bowl and put aside. Pour sauce over salad when serving.

Serves 4–6

TOMATO SALAD

4 tomatoes, cubed
1 stick celery, chopped
2 fresh green chillies *or* ½
   capsicum, chopped
Salt
1 tablespoon lemon juice

Mix tomatoes, celery and chillies gently in a bowl. Sprinkle over salt to taste and lemon juice, and mix gently.
Serve with any curry.

Serves 4–6

CUCUMBER AND PINEAPPLE SALAD

1 large cucumber, peeled
and sliced or diced
1 cup canned pineapple
cubes with syrup *or*
canned crushed pineapple
with syrup *or* fresh
pineapple cubes
1 small onion, minced
1 fresh green chilli *or* ½
capsicum, minced coarsely
Pinch salt

In a glass salad bowl, combine cucumber, pineapple cubes with syrup, minced onion, green chillies and salt.
Chill and serve with rice and curry or Pilau (p. 74).

Serves 4–6

CUCUMBER AND TOMATO SALAD

1 large cucumber, peeled
and sliced or diced
2 ripe tomatoes, sliced or
diced
1 small onion, minced or
sliced finely
1 tablespoon lime juice *or* 1
tablespoon vinegar mixed
with 1 teaspoon sugar
Salt

In a bowl, mix cucumber, tomatoes and onion.
Add lime juice and salt to taste. Mix gently. Chill in the refrigerator until required.
Serve with Pilau (p. 74) or any curry.

Serves 4–6

CUCUMBER, ONION AND CELERY SALAD

1 large cucumber, peeled
and sliced
1 large onion, sliced finely
3 stalks celery, minced or
chopped finely
1 tablespoon chilli sauce *or* 2
tablespoons tomato sauce

Arrange cucumber rings and onion on a platter or in a bowl and sprinkle minced celery over. Keep in the refrigerator until required.
When serving, pour chilli sauce or tomato sauce over salad.
Serve with Pilau (p. 74) or any curry.

Serves 4–6

YOGHURT WITH CUCUMBER

1 tablespoon cooking oil
¼ teaspoon mustard seed
Pinch fenugreek
1 small onion, chopped
    finely
Thin slice ginger, chopped
    finely
2 cups natural yoghurt
1 cucumber, peeled, seeded,
    and chopped into small
    cubes
Salt

Heat oil in frying pan and fry mustard seed and fenugreek for 2 seconds only, then add onion and fry until golden brown.
Add ginger, fry for 2 seconds only and remove pan from heat.
Pour yoghurt into a bowl and add the fried ingredients, cucumber, and salt to taste.
Stir well and keep aside in the refrigerator until ready to serve.
Serve cold.
Serve with curry and rice, bread or Yellow Rice (p. 72).

YOGHURT WITH CHOKO

Make as for Yoghurt with Cucumber (p. 89) but for the cucumber substitute a large choko, peeled, cut into small cubes, boiled until soft and drained.

SPICED YOGHURT

1½ tablespoons oil
¼ teaspoon mustard seed
Pinch fenugreek
1 small onion, chopped
    finely
2 cloves garlic, chopped
    finely
2 dry red chillies, cut into 15
    mm (½ in) pieces
¼ teaspoon cummin
1 fresh green chilli, chopped
    finely
3 curry leaves
Salt
2 cups natural yoghurt,
    beaten well

Heat oil in a frying pan, add mustard seed and fry for 2 seconds only. Add fenugreek, then onions and fry until golden brown.
Lower heat, then add garlic, dry chillies, cummin, green chilli, curry leaves and salt to taste. Stir for 5 seconds and remove pan from heat.
Add beaten yoghurt, mix well and pour into a bowl. Do not boil yoghurt.
Chill in refrigerator.
Serve cold with plain rice or Yellow Rice (p. 72), and with any curry.

Serves 4–6

BANANA AND COCONUT SALAD

Bananas
Desiccated coconut
Lemon juice (optional)

Peel required number of bananas (allow half a small banana per person), and slice thinly.
Sprinkle desiccated coconut over banana and gently mix until all slices are well covered with coconut.
Serve within an hour of cutting banana, or it may brown or, if liked, sprinkle banana rings with lemon juice before rolling in coconut, to stop the browning.
Serve with any curry.

SALAD COCKTAIL

12 lettuce leaves
1 cucumber, peeled and sliced
2 tomatoes, sliced
3 hard-boiled eggs, sliced
500 g (1 lb) cooked prawns seasoned with pepper and salt to taste (optional)
½–1 cup canned or fresh pineapple cubes
Salad dressing of choice

Arrange lettuce leaves around the edge of a flat plate. Make a second circle of cucumber slices, then a circle of tomato slices, then a ring of egg slices, then of cooked prawns, if used. Pile pineapple cubes in the centre.
Sprinkle whole with a little salad dressing.

Serves 4–6

CHUTNEYS, PICKLES AND SAUCES

Chutneys and pickles are very important curry accompaniments. In India, 'chutneys' are blended vegetables and fruits which must be served immediately or within a week if kept in the refrigerator. 'Pickles' are what people in Western countries often call chutneys—cooked fruit and vegetable sauces which have great keeping properties and can be kept many months when bottled and sealed. Some chutneys and pickles are hot, some sweet and fruity, others tangy or spicy. It is a good idea to serve more than one type at a meal, especially if one is very hot. Remember that the chillies added to the chutney or pickle control the heat—cut the chilli content down or increase it, as desired.

The chutneys given here are of many different types. Many are made of fresh, uncooked ingredients, and most must be used within a few days of making. A blender is very useful in making those chutneys which should be smooth. The pickles are designed to keep and should be bottled in sterilised jars, sealed, labelled and dated.

The sauces at the end of this chapter may be used as dips, or to accompany grills and fried meats. Of course, many of the dishes in earlier chapters have their own sauces, which may be made and used separately in this way also, if desired.

It is a good idea to have one or two commercial chutneys or pickles, and a few sauces, on hand for use when time presses, and to provide variety. Marvellous products may now be found in specialty shops and the supermarket shelves.

MINT CHUTNEY

30 mint leaves, washed, drained and chopped or minced
1 small onion, chopped or minced
3 fresh green chillies, chopped or minced
Thin slice ginger, chopped or minced
2 tablespoons lemon juice *or* vinegar
Salt

Put chopped mint leaves, onion, green chillies and ginger into a blender. Blend to a smooth paste. Alternatively, grind minced mint, onion, chillies and ginger thoroughly in mortar, to make a smooth paste.
Remove paste to a bowl, add lemon juice or vinegar and salt to taste and mix well.
Keep in the refrigerator until required.
Serve with rice and curry or use on bread for sandwiches. Also good with Pilau (p. 74).

RED TOMATO CHUTNEY

6 large red tomatoes, diced
1 large onion, diced
2 celery leaves, chopped
 finely
½ capsicum, chopped finely
2 teaspoons sugar
1 tablespoon lime juice *or*
 vinegar
Salt

Mix all ingredients in a glass bowl, and store in refrigerator until required.
Serve with Yellow Rice (p. 72) or curry.

GREEN APPLE CHUTNEY

2 green apples, peeled and
 grated
Salt
1 teaspoon sugar (or more to
 taste)
1 large onion, finely minced
2 fresh green chillies, finely
 minced
½ capsicum, finely minced
1 tablespoon lemon juice *or*
 vinegar

In a glass bowl, mix together grated apples, salt to taste, sugar, onion, chillies and capsicum.
Add lemon juice or vinegar and mix well.
Chill in the refrigerator until required.
Serve with Pilau, (p. 74) rice or curry.

APPLE AND PINEAPPLE CHUTNEY

½ cup strong white vinegar
½ cup sugar
2 green apples, peeled and
 chopped finely
½ cup raisins
1 clove garlic, sliced finely
4 fresh green chillies *or*
 1 capsicum, sliced thickly
½ teaspoon cinnamon
3 cups canned crushed
 pineapple
Pinch salt

In a saucepan, mix vinegar and sugar and bring slowly to the boil.
Add apple, raisins, garlic, chillies or capsicum and cinnamon. Mix well. Bring back to boil and boil slowly until apple is soft and broken, stirring constantly.
Add pineapple and salt, bring back to the boil, reduce heat, and simmer, stirring, until chutney thickens.
Remove from heat and leave to cool. Pour into a jar and store in the refrigerator. This chutney will keep for a week.
Serve with rice, curry or with roast meat, but best with vegetarian dishes.

CELERY OR CORIANDER LEAF CHUTNEY

30 stalks Chinese celery *or* coriander leaves, chopped or minced
3 fresh green chillies, chopped or minced
Thin slice ginger, chopped or minced
1 clove garlic (optional), crushed
1 tablespoon lemon juice *or* vinegar
Salt

Put chopped Chinese celery or coriander leaves, chillies, ginger, and garlic (optional) into a blender and blend to make a paste. Alternatively, grind minced Chinese celery or coriander, chillies, ginger and garlic (optional) in mortar, until mixture is as smooth as possible.

Transfer paste to a bowl, add lemon juice or vinegar and salt to taste. Mix well and keep in the refrigerator until required.

Serve with Yellow Rice (p. 72) or Vegetable Rice (p. 72).

COCONUT CHUTNEY

1 cup desiccated coconut
4 fresh green chillies, chopped or minced
1 small onion, chopped or minced
½ teaspoon tamarind paste *or* lemon juice
2 tablespoons water
Salt

Put desiccated coconut, chopped chillies, chopped onion, tamarind paste and water into a blender and blend until mixture is smooth. Alternatively, grind coconut, minced chillies, minced onion, tamarind paste and water in a mortar, until mixture is a smooth paste.

Transfer paste to a bowl, add salt to taste and keep in the refrigerator until serving time.

Serve with Dosa (p. 21) or Yellow Rice (p. 72).

RAISIN AND TOMATO CHUTNEY

½ cup raisins, pounded into a paste
3 ripe tomatoes, diced
1 small onion, minced finely
2 fresh green chillies *or* ½ capsicum, minced finely
Thin slice ginger, pounded
1½ tablespoons vinegar
1 teaspoon sugar
Salt

In a bowl, mix together raisin paste, tomatoes, onion, chillies or capsicum and ginger.

Add vinegar, sugar and salt to taste. Mix well or blend to make a fine, smooth paste.

Store in the refrigerator until required. Will keep for about 2 days.

Serve with rice, roast meat, or curry.

RAISIN AND MANGO CHUTNEY

Make as for Raisin and Tomato Chutney (p. 93), but substitute mangoes, peeled and diced, for tomatoes.

MANGO PICKLE

5 medium mangoes, peeled and minced
1 cup white sugar
$\frac{1}{2}$ cup white vinegar
5 mm ($\frac{1}{4}$ in) slice ginger, pounded
2 teaspoons chilli powder
Salt

Put minced mangoes in a saucepan and add sugar, vinegar, pounded ginger, chilli powder and salt to taste. Mix well, bring to the boil and boil slowly for 10 minutes.
Reduce heat to low, and continue to stir and cook until mangoes are soft and the mixture is jam-like in consistency.
Remove from heat, leave to cool, pour into a sterilised bottle, and seal.
Serve with rice, roast meat, curry or puris.

LEMON AND DATE PICKLE

$\frac{1}{2}$ cup cooking oil
$\frac{1}{2}$ teaspoon mustard seed, crushed
75 mm (3 in) piece ginger, pounded
1 ripe lemon, boiled for about 30 seconds and cut into 15 mm ($\frac{1}{2}$ in) cubes
10 seedless dates, chopped finely
1 tablespoon paprika *or* chilli powder (for those who like it hot)
Salt to taste
Pinch cinnamon powder
$\frac{1}{2}$ cup vinegar
2 tablespoons brown sugar

Heat oil in a frying pan, add mustard powder and fry for 2 seconds only.
Reduce heat to low and add all other ingredients. Mix well, bring to the boil, and boil for 10 minutes.
Remove from heat and leave to cool. Pour into a sterilised jar and seal.
Serve with Pilau (p. 74) or Vegetable Rice (p. 72).

LEMON PICKLE

Make as for Lemon and Date Pickle (p. 94), but omit dates and substitute ½ teaspoon asafoetida powder for cinnamon.

TOMATO PICKLE

3 tomatoes, ripe or green, chopped or minced
4 fresh green chillies, chopped or minced
1 clove garlic crushed (optional)
½ teaspoon sugar
Salt
Thin slice of ginger, chopped or shredded finely
1 small onion, chopped or minced
3 tablespoons vinegar
Pinch citric acid

Put tomatoes, chillies, garlic, sugar, salt to taste, ginger, onion and vinegar into a blender and blend until mixture is smooth.

Alternatively, grind minced tomatoes, minced chillies, crushed garlic, sugar, salt, shredded ginger, minced onion and vinegar in mortar until mixture is as smooth as possible.

Remove mixture to a saucepan. Bring to the boil, reduce heat and simmer, stirring all the time, until mixture thickens.

Remove from heat, cool, and add citric acid. Stir well, pour into a sterilised bottle, and seal.

Serve with Yellow Rice (p. 72).

AUBERGINE PICKLE

3 large aubergines (egg-plants) sliced finely
1 teaspoon turmeric
6 cloves, crushed
½ teaspoon cummin
1 teaspoon chilli powder
½ teaspoon mustard seed, pounded coarsely
½ cup white vinegar
2 teaspoons brown sugar
Salt
3 tablespoons cooking oil

In a bowl, mix sliced aubergines and turmeric and put aside.

In another bowl, mix crushed cloves, cummin, chilli powder, mustard seed, vinegar, brown sugar and salt to taste. Mix into a paste and put aside.

Heat oil in a frying pan and fry sliced aubergines, stirring, until lightly browned. Drain and put aside.

Add the mixed spice paste to the same oil and fry on low heat for about 10 minutes.

Add the fried aubergines, mix well, and fry for a further 10 minutes until soft, then remove from heat and cool.

Pour into a sterilised jar, seal, and keep in the refrigerator until required.

Serve with rice and curry.

SPICY SAUCE

1 tablespoon cooking oil
1 onion, chopped finely
2 cloves garlic, crushed
1 cup tomato sauce
½ teaspoon worcestershire
   sauce
1 tablespoon chilli sauce
   (optional)
125 g (4 oz) canned
   pineapple pieces
1 tablespoon vinegar
2 teaspoons sugar

Heat oil in frying pan, add chopped onions and garlic and fry until lightly browned.

Reduce heat to low and add tomato sauce, worcestershire sauce, chilli sauce (optional), and pineapple pieces. Mix well, bring to the boil, reduce heat and boil slowly, stirring for 5 minutes. Remove from heat and pour into a bowl.

Good as a dip with Fried Meat Balls (p. 19).

Serves 4–6

SATAY SAUCE

2 tablespoons cooking oil
1 onion, chopped finely
2 cloves garlic, crushed
½ teaspoon shrimp paste
1½ tablespoons coriander *or*
   curry powder
½ teaspoon chilli powder
   (optional)
¼ teaspoon aniseed
¼ teaspoon cummin
1 stalk lemon grass, pounded
   or chopped
6 buttons candlenut,
   pounded into a paste
1 cup roasted peanuts,
   pounded coarsely *or* 6
   tablespoons crunchy
   peanut butter
1 teaspoon sugar
6 tablespoons tamarind juice
   or 1 tablespoon tamarind
   paste
125 g (4 oz) coconut cream
Salt

In a frying pan, heat oil and fry onions until golden brown.

Reduce heat to low and add garlic, shrimp paste, coriander, chilli powder (optional), aniseed, cummin, lemon grass and candlenut paste and fry, stirring, for 10 minutes, until fragrant.

Add ground nuts and sugar, stirring slowly. Fry for 5 minutes, then add tamarind juice, coconut cream and salt to taste and fry until oil rises.

Remove from heat and serve with grilled Satay (p. 62), sliced cucumber and onion rings.

Serves 4–6

GINGER SAUCE

1½ tablespoons peanut oil
½ teaspoon mustard seed
3 or 4 curry leaves
1 small onion, chopped
    finely
50 mm (2 in) piece ginger,
    shredded or minced
1½ teaspoons coriander or
    curry powder
1 fresh green chilli (optional)
Salt
1 teaspoon sugar
2 tablespoons tamarind
    water or 1 teaspoon
    tamarind paste

Heat peanut oil in a pan, add mustard seed and curry leaves, then add onions and fry till golden brown.

Add ginger, coriander, chilli (optional), salt to taste, sugar and tamarind water or paste. Mix well. Bring to the boil, reduce heat, and boil slowly until oil rises. Remove from heat and pour into a dish to cool.

Serve with Spicy Chicken and Rice Porridge (p. 42) and Pilau (p. 74).

KABAB SAUCE

1 large onion, minced
Thin slice ginger, pounded
5 stalks fresh mint, pounded
1 fresh green chilli, pounded
1 tablespoon fresh lemon
    juice
Salt to taste

Mix all ingredients in a bowl, or place in a blender, and blend into a sauce.
Store in the refrigerator until needed.
Serve with Kabab (p. 61).

Serves 4–6

Note: If a hotter sauce is required, increase the number of chillies to 3 or 4.

DESSERTS

This chapter includes many delicious desserts which provide a refreshing finish to any meal, particularly a spicy Indian one. The recipes in this chapter fall into three basic sections—cool and decorative fruit desserts, smooth Indian puddings, based on milk, and sweets, ideal to serve with coffee. The fruit desserts will, I hope, give you some new ideas, but almost any combination of fresh or canned fruit may be tried.

If you do not wish to make a dessert, consider some of the following ideas to round off your Indian meal:

A platter of fresh fruit—grapes, slices of melon, strawberries, pineapple, mangoes, pawpaw and lychees, if available.

A selection of Indian sweets, available in specialty shops, with chocolate, and perhaps some almonds and muscatel grapes.

Natural or flavoured yoghurt, with fresh or canned fruit or plain.

Really good, full cream ice-cream, plain or flavoured.

A selection of nuts in the shell, with glace fruits, and dried fruits such as figs, dates and apricots.

LYCHEES WITH HONEYDEW MELON

3 cups honeydew melon, scooped into balls
1 can lychees with syrup

Mix fruits and syrup together. Chill.
Serve plain or with ice-cream.

Serves 6–8

Note: This and the following fruit desserts look most attractive served in a glass bowl.

LYCHEES WITH MIXED FRUITS

1 can lychees, drained *or* 12 fresh lychees, peeled
1 can fruit cocktail (fruit salad) with syrup
2 mandarin oranges (tangerines), peeled and cubed

Mix fruits and syrup together. Chill.
Serve plain or with ice-cream.

Serves 4–6

Carrot Pudding (p. 102) and Vermicelli Pudding (p. 102).

MIXED FRUITS SALAD

2 cups canned pineapple
   cubes with syrup
1 red apple, peeled, if
   desired, and diced
1 cup fresh cherries *or* fresh
   seedless or seeded grapes
1 pear, peeled and diced

Mix fruits and syrup together. Chill.
Serve plain or with ice-cream.

Serves 4–6

MELON DESSERT

1 can fruit cocktail (fruit
   salad) with syrup
2 bananas, sliced or diced
1 cup watermelon, scooped
   into balls
1 cup rockmelon
   (canteloupe), scooped into
   balls

Mix fruits and syrup together. Chill.
Serve plain or with ice-cream or whipped fresh
cream.

Serves 4–6

FRUIT SALAD WITH ALMOND JELLY

15 g (½ oz) Chinese grass
   jelly *or* powder jelly
3 cups water
1½ cups sugar
2 drops almond essence
½ cup evaporated milk
1 can of fruit cocktail (fruit
   salad) with syrup *or* fresh
   fruit salad

In a saucepan mix grass jelly or powder jelly, water
and sugar, and bring to the boil.
Boil gently and stir until sugar is dissolved and then
leave to boil for 10 minutes, stirring occasionally to
prevent boiling over.
Add almond essence, remove from heat, and
slowly add evaporated milk, stirring.
Return to heat, bring to the boil and boil for 5
seconds only, remove and pour in a jelly mould or
bowl.
Allow to cool for 10 minutes, then put in the
refrigerator to set.
When ready to serve, unmould or cut into desired
shapes and serve with fruit cocktail or fresh fruit
salad.

Serves 4–6

Semolina Halwa (p. 104), Halwa (p. 103) and Semolina
Cookies (p. 103).

JELLY WITH LONGANS

1 packet jelly crystals (any
  flavour)
1 can longans with syrup
1 sweet apple, peeled, if
  desired, and diced
1 pear, peeled and diced
1 cup canned pineapple
  cubes, drained *or* fresh
  pineapple cubes

Prepare jelly following instructions on the packet,
pour into a glass bowl and chill until set.
Mix longans, apple, pear and pineapple cubes. Pile
on top of jelly.
Serve with whipped cream or ice-cream.

Serves 4–6

BANANA FRITTERS

1 cup plain flour
Pinch salt
1 egg, beaten
1 small can evaporated milk
4 bananas
1 cup cooking oil
½ cup castor sugar

Sift flour and salt into a bowl. Make a well in the
centre of the flour, and into this pour the beaten
egg.
Blend the egg with a little flour at a time by stirring
in gradually increasing circles from the centre.
As mixture thickens, add milk gradually, while
continuing to stir, to form a smooth batter.
Allow to stand for 30 minutes.
Split bananas in half lengthwise.
Heat oil in a frying pan over moderate heat.
Dip bananas in the batter and add to the pan, deep
frying until golden brown.
Remove, drain well, and roll in castor sugar.
Serve with cream.

BANANA COCONUT PUDDING
Bubor cha cha

4 cups water
4 tablespoons sago
2 tablespoons brown sugar
1 tablespoon white sugar
125 g (4 oz) coconut cream
4 bananas, sliced
10 cherries, stoned and
  chopped coarsely
½ cup evaporated milk
Pinch salt

In a saucepan, bring 3 cups of the water to the boil.
Add sago, brown sugar and white sugar and stir,
then slowly add coconut cream and remaining 1
cup water, stirring all the time. Bring to the boil,
reduce heat and boil slowly, stirring, until sago is
cooked.
Add banana rings, cherries, evaporated milk and
salt. Stir gently for 5 minutes and remove from
heat. Pour into a serving dish. Serve hot or cold.

Serves 6

SAGO AND SWEET POTATO PUDDING

2 cups sweet potato, diced
4 cups water
½ cup brown sugar
2 tablespoons white sugar
Pinch salt
½ cup sago
125 g (4 oz) coconut cream
6 tablespoons evaporated
   milk

Put diced sweet potato and water into a saucepan, bring to the boil, cover, and continue to boil until sweet potato is cooked.
Add brown sugar, white sugar and salt. Mix well. Reduce heat to moderate, and add sago while stirring. Bring to the boil, and boil for 10 minutes. When sago is cooked add coconut cream, mix well, bring back to the boil and boil for 5 minutes. Remove from heat, add evaporated milk and mix well. Pour into serving dish. Serve hot or cold.

Serves 4–6

RICE PUDDING

2 cups cooked rice
1 cup water
½ cup sugar
Pinch salt
125 g (4 oz) coconut cream
1¼ cups milk
1 tablespoon butter
125 g (4 oz) almonds,
   chopped
2 tablespoons raisins

Put rice and water into a saucepan. Bring to boil, boil rapidly until rice is soft and broken up.
Reduce heat to moderate and add sugar, salt, coconut cream and milk and stir. Bring to the boil, boil for 5 minutes and remove from heat.
In a frying pan, heat butter, fry almonds until light brown, add raisins and fry until raisins swell.
Pour almonds and raisins into rice pudding, and stir well. If pudding is too thick more milk can be added. Pour into a serving dish.
Serve hot as a dessert or for breakfast.

Serves 4

SWEET POTATO PUDDING

5 tablespoons sugar
2 eggs, beaten well
Pinch salt
2 drops vanilla essence
125 g (4 oz) butter *or* ghee
3 tablespoons custard
   powder
125 g (4 oz) coconut cream
   mixed with 1 cup water
½ cup evaporated milk
2 cups boiled, mashed sweet
   potatoes

In a bowl, mix sugar, beaten eggs, salt, vanilla essence and 60 g (2 oz) of the butter. Cream well. Add custard powder, coconut cream and water, evaporated milk and mashed sweet potatoes. Mix well with a wooden spoon to a smooth batter.
Grease an ovenproof dish or baking tin and pour mixture into it. Dot remaining 60 g (2 oz) butter on top and bake (180°C, 350°F) until pudding sets.
Cut and serve warm or cold.

Serves 6

CARROT PUDDING

185 g (6 oz) ghee *or* butter
  (or more if needed)
500 g (1 lb) carrots,
  shredded finely
½ teaspoon cardamom
  powder
250 g (8 oz) sugar
250 g (8 oz) evaporated milk
  or fresh milk
3 tablespoons shredded
  blanched almonds
2 tablespoons blanched
  pistachio nuts (optional)
2 drops rose essence
125 g (4 oz) roasted cashew
  nuts

Heat ghee in a saucepan on moderate heat, add shredded carrots and cardamom powder, mix well, and cook for 10 minutes, uncovered.
Add sugar and milk. Mix well and bring to the boil.
Add shredded almonds, pistachio nuts (optional) and rose essence. Reduce heat, simmer, stirring constantly, until mixture is very thick and leaves the sides of the saucepan.
Spread mixture evenly on a flat plate and sprinkle with roasted cashew nuts.
Serve hot or cold.

Serves 6

VERMICELLI PUDDING

2 tablespoons ghee *or*
  butter
3 cardamom pods, crushed
  or pinch cardamom
  powder
170 g (6 oz) thin vermicelli
2 cups water
1 cup sugar
1 drop yellow food
  colouring (optional)
60 g (2 oz) almonds,
  chopped and fried lightly
125 g (4 oz) cashew nuts,
  fried lightly
30 g (1 oz) pistachio nuts,
  chopped (optional)
2 drops vanilla essence
4 cups milk *or* 2 cups
  evaporated milk mixed
  with 2 cups water

Heat ghee or butter in a saucepan over a low heat, add cardamom and fry for 2 seconds only.
Add vermicelli and fry until light brown in colour, stirring often.
Add water and sugar, boil for 10 minutes over moderate heat, then add yellow colouring (optional), fried almonds, fried cashew nuts, pistachio nuts (optional) and vanilla essence. Mix well.
Reduce heat to low, add milk or evaporated milk, stir, bring to the boil and remove from heat. Pour into a serving dish.
Serve hot or cold.

Serves 4–6

Note: If desired, lightly fried raisins may be added with the nuts.

SEMOLINA COOKIES

2 cups plain flour
$\frac{1}{4}$ cup semolina
1 cup sugar
$\frac{1}{4}$ teaspoon bicarbonate of
  soda
155 g (5 oz) ghee (or more
  if needed)

In a bowl, mix flour, semolina, sugar and bicarbonate of soda.

Melt ghee and add little at a time to the bowl, kneading the mixture to a soft dough.

Form mixture into balls the size of a large marble and place them on baking sheets or trays, leaving 40 mm (1$\frac{1}{2}$ in) space between them.

Preheat oven (180°C, 350°F) and bake the cookies for 20 minutes. Cookies will not brown, but will move freely on the tray when cooked.

Remove from oven and allow the cookies to cool on the trays. When cold, store in air-tight bottles.

Yield: 40–44

HALWA

4 cups white sugar
$\frac{1}{2}$ pint water
1 cup cornflour
2 drops yellow colouring
$\frac{1}{2}$ teaspoon rose essence
1 teaspoon lemon juice
4 tablespoons ghee *or* butter
  (or more if needed)
Pinch cardamom powder
  (optional)
2 tablespoons shredded,
  blanched almonds (or
  more if desired)
2 tablespoons pistachio nuts

Put sugar and water in a saucepan, bring to the boil, reduce heat and boil slowly, stirring, for 5 minutes until sugar dissolves.

Remove saucepan from heat, slowly add cornflour, stirring all the time.

Add yellow colouring and rose essence and mix well. Return to heat and cook over moderate heat, stirring continuously, until mixture turns into a lump.

Add lemon juice and stir again, then add ghee, cardamom powder (optional), 2 tablespoons shredded almonds and pistachio nuts. Stir for a further 10 minutes.

When mixture leaves the side of the saucepan, remove from heat. Pour on to a well-greased flat plate. Extra shredded almonds can be sprinkled on top, if desired.

When cooled, cut halwa into diamond-shaped pieces, cubes, or desired shapes.

Serves 6

SEMOLINA HALWA

250 g (8 oz) ghee *or* butter
  (or more if needed)
½ teaspoon cardamom
  powder
2 cups semolina
1 cup water
2 cups sugar
2 drops yellow colouring
125 g (4 oz) blanched
  almonds, chopped
125 g (4 oz) cashew nuts
125 g (4 oz) raisins

In a saucepan, heat ghee, add cardamom powder and semolina and fry for 5 minutes.

Add water and sugar and stir until sugar is dissolved.

Reduce heat to low, and continue cooking and stirring until mixture begins to leave the sides of the saucepan, then add yellow colouring.

Add almonds, cashews and raisins and mix well.

Fry for another 5 minutes, adding more ghee if required and remove from heat.

Spread mixture on a greased plate, and press smooth. Put aside to cool.

When halwa is cold, cut into small pieces and serve.

INDEX